Road Trip

Five Adventures
You're Meant to Live

A Modern Girl's Bible Study
Refreshingly Unique

JEN HATMAKER

NavPress is the publishing ministry of The Navigators, an international Christian organization and leader in personal spiritual development. NavPress is committed to helping people grow spiritually and enjoy lives of meaning and hope through personal and group resources that are biblically rooted, culturally relevant, and highly practical.

For a free catalog go to www.NavPress.com or call 1.800.366.7788 in the United States or 1.800.839.4769 in Canada.

www.navpress.com

ISBN 978-1-57683-892-1

Cover design by Wes Youssi, The DesignWorks Group
Cover photo by David Stuart
Creative Team: Terry Behimer, Karen Lee-Thorp, Collette Knittel, Kathy Mosier, Arvid Wallen, Bob Bubnis

Some of the anecdotal illustrations in this book are true to life and are included with the permission of the persons involved. All other illustrations are composites of real situations, and any resemblance to people living or dead is coincidental.

Printed in the United States of America

6 7 8 9 10 11 / 17 16 15 14

Holy Spirit, this has to go to You.
I thought I knew You well before, but You've taken me to brand new places. For enlarging Your Word and stretching my experience, I love You. Thank You for being such an extraordinary Teacher. You are my secure confidence.

Contents

Acknowledgments 9

Introduction 11

WEEK ONE: ROAD TRIP

DAY 1 No Parking: Life Is a Trip 15

DAY 2 Road Narrows Ahead: Chart Your Course 21

DAY 3 Dumping Grounds: Travel Light 27

DAY 4 HOV Lane: Travel Together 33

DAY 5 Rest Stop 39

WEEK TWO: IDENTITY (Samaritan Woman at the Well)

DAY 1 Road Block One: Culture 45

DAY 2 Road Block Two: Gender 51

DAY 3 Road Block Three: Sin 57

DAY 4 The Road Is Cleared 62

DAY 5 Rest Stop 66

WEEK THREE: FAITH (Abram)

DAY 1 Step One: Baby Steps 71

DAY 2 Step Two: Beware of Alternate Routes 78

DAY 3 Step Three: Embrace the Delays 83

DAY 4 Step Four: The Bridge of Sacrifice 88
DAY 5 Rest Stop 93

WEEK FOUR: DISCIPLESHIP (PETER)

DAY 1 Leaving the Nets 99
DAY 2 Follow the Rabbi 105
DAY 3 A New Rock 110
DAY 4 A Commissioning 116
DAY 5 Rest Stop 121

WEEK FIVE: CONTENTMENT (PAUL)

DAY 1 Insatiable 127
DAY 2 Appetite 134
DAY 3 The Secret 140
DAY 4 Ravenous 147
DAY 5 Rest Stop 152

WEEK SIX: SERVICE (THE CHURCH)

DAY 1 The Estate 157
DAY 2 Holy Fire 163
DAY 3 The Circle of the Gifted 167
DAY 4 The Clear Winner 173
DAY 5 Rest Stop 178

Leader's Guide 181
Notes 185
About the Author 189

Acknowledgments

I must thank my husband, Brandon, and our three bundles, Gavin, Sydney Beth, and Caleb. During this writing, our home fell on some hard times. Namely, complete and utter neglect. For wearing dirty socks and eating pizza four nights a week, I love you. Brandon, thank you for reminding me when I wore the same clothes two days in a row or more. That's the kind of accountability you knew I needed. This is why we're partners for life.

I need to thank my Girlfriends Trina and Leslie, who played the martyrs' role of getting their brains picked on subject matter. My questions were relentless. You endured like warriors. Thank you for your counsel, your opinions, and your enthusiasm—feigned or not. For the endless breakfast tacos and the holy oil of friendship, I love you.

For my dear Thursday night Bible study Girlfriends, thank you for allowing me to bow out for a spell so I could write. And thank you for collectively putting the screws to me once again to come back. There's nothing quite like adult peer pressure. You are my favorite girls, and I love you.

Heartfelt thanks goes to my editor, Karen Lee-Thorp. You really earned your stripes on this road trip. For wearing all the hats—cheerleader, coach, teacher, mother—I'm so thankful. There is no way you get paid enough. I'm also grateful to Terry

Behimer with NavPress who gently helped make a transition last summer. For picking up the banner, moving forward, and enlarging my boundaries, thanks. You two have given me the freedom to write like I do, meticulous accountability, and experienced counsel. Editors rule.

And to Mom, thanks for pimping me out to everyone you know. I'm positive your friends and colleagues are sick of you. So for the two hundred people that will buy my stuff under complete duress, thank you. A thirty-one-year-old is still happy to make her Mama proud.

Introduction

Welcome to this crazy Road Trip! You're in for quite a ride! You are in the right place if you want to (1) learn, (2) grow, (3) laugh, (4) change, or (5) discover you're not the only Modern Girl out there. This is an adventure for you. The thing about us Modern Girls is that we just are who we are. We're not trying to be like our mothers or, heaven forbid, our grandmothers. We envy our girlfriends and get our hair highlighted. We might watch *American Idol.* When our generation approaches God, it has to be real. Don't try to sell us churchy stereotypes or a prepackaged relationship.

I believe God wants our spiritual journey to be as fun as it is authentic. To that end, I am a zealot for God's Word. After many years of mind-numbing VBS and Sunday school with eighty-five-year-old teachers who made the Bible the most boring waste of time on the planet (God bless 'em), I finally discovered that the Word is actually a fascinating place. Who knew? Evidently, it's even relevant. I hope you conclude the same.

So as you put the car in drive with this Modern Girl, I wanted to touch on a couple of things. We'll study five mega-themes necessary for a healthy spirit. These are the nonnegotiables of true progress. A sustained neglect of any of these will derail your growth in one way or another. Having said that, I always find it annoying when the author of a Bible study tries to make an issue for me that I don't have. I squeeze my eyes shut and think, *How has my dad wronged me? There's* got *to be something!* Listen, as we journey together, if I touch on a subpoint that's not your issue, don't sweat it. Don't force drama where there is none. By the same turn, if a "check in your spirit" pops up, as my Girlfriend Leah says, spend some time there digging it out with the help of the Holy Spirit. In these five areas, it's likely you're doing fine in one and struggling in another. So if you discover your own spiritual health along the way, celebrate it and concentrate on the areas you need to move forward in.

In addition to this book, you'll need a lined journal and a Bible. I mostly used the NIV, but Girl, do your own thing. I'm not your boss. Just your fellow Modern Girl.

You'll encounter three icons throughout the study representing three different ways to respond. The radio icon indicates a time to dig into the Word, the rearview mirror icon offers a chance to personally reflect on truth, and the telephone icon opens the door to intimate prayer.

Enjoy the ride.

WEEK ONE

Road Trip

DAY ONE

No Parking: Life Is a Trip

My first real road trip was the summer after my freshman year in college. My three best friends—Andrea, Katie, and Stacy—and I decided we had reached the peak of maturity at 19, we had cash to blow, and we were entitled to a road trip. We'd grown up in Kansas and had basically been nowhere. So we put our heads of enormous hair together and dreamed. We dreamed large. We were going places. We were going to hit the open highway and head to . . . Dallas! I'm just saying no one lived on the edge like we did. We were travelers. *Sojourners* really.

So with a wave out the window of Stacy's mom's minivan and a squeal of our tires, we were off to The Big D. We road tripped like veterans. We saw every major attraction. We were up early and out late (behaving, of course). We budgeted to squeeze everything in. We laughed until we were sick. We took pictures we'd all like to forget. We left our mark. I'll be honest: I don't think Dallas was ever the same after us. They're probably still talking about The Weekend the Girls Came Down.

And when we returned to Kansas, we were all a little wiser. We had *seen things*, I tell you. We would never again be content just staying put. Moving forward, adding layers, growing and changing—this was our mantra. Life was a Road Trip, and we planned to enjoy the ride.

Today, I'm older. I've experienced more. I've traveled to other countries and Vegas. More significantly, I've traveled spiritually. Much to my surprise, I've discovered that my Girlfriends and I were right. Life *is* a road trip. God designed it that way. As it turns out, His plan all along was for us to grow. Progress. Travel ahead. Mature. Develop. Change. Expand. See more. Do more. Experience more. Become more.

The way I know this is simple: God repeated Himself enough times in the Bible for even the dullest student to catch His drift. This is how many times the following words or phrases appear in Scripture:

- grow—71
- journey—56
- go forward—52
- move—51
- advance—42
- travel—33 (MSG)
- mature—24 (MSG)

Do you see where God is going with this? He is completely about spiritual progression. I can empathize with God's position here as "Father." It's the Parent Factor. My youngest son, Caleb, just turned three. If you told me he would never grow up and would remain exactly as he is now, I'd get in my SUV and drive myself straight to LoonyLand where they could make it all go away with the pretty little pills.

Don't get me wrong: I love him. Many of his antics are endearing, but only because we know them to be *temporary*. To be fair, he acts like a toddler because he is one. If he is still riding his scooter down the street buck naked in twenty years, then we'll have a real problem (as if we don't have one now). But truthfully, I sometimes daydream about when he's older, perhaps rational. When we can take Caleb's fun personality and add maturity, we're going to throw a party and get new carpet.

We are God's children in the same exact sense. He allows us a period of infancy in our relationship with Him either because we're literally young, or we're spiritually young as all new believers are.

In Matthew 11:28, Jesus spoke some of my favorite words: "Come to me, all you who are weary and burdened, and I will give you rest." In verse 25, He described those He was talking to as "little children."

Matthew Henry said, "Some of the greatest scholars and the greatest statesmen have been the greatest strangers to gospel mysteries. . . . We must thank God that they are 'revealed to babes'; that the meek and humble are beautified with this salvation; and this honor put upon those whom the world pours contempt upon."[1] Just as with my Caleb, many of our qualities are endearing to God in our spiritual infancy. He plucks those out and urges us to keep them while the rest of our spirit matures.

What childlike traits does God want us to *maintain* throughout our journey?

Matthew 18:2-4

Matthew 21:16

Mark 10:13-16

1 Peter 2:2

*Are any of these a struggle for you? Why?

In our humility and simplicity, we will learn from our gentle Savior. He promises that. Just like a parent of a toddler, He cares for us uniquely during the early stages of growth. God spends time patiently teaching the spiritually young, whether in age or commitment. Jesus cried over Jerusalem in Luke 13:34: "How often I have longed to gather your children together, as a hen gathers her chicks under her wings." This is Jesus. Gentle Teacher, Fierce Protector.

But salvation is only the beginning of the Road Trip.

*Compare God's role as Parent to our role as parents. From that perspective, list three or four reasons why God might desire growth in His children. Why would you want *your* kids to grow up?

You know what I look forward to? Some of the same things God does:

1. *A mature relationship with my kids.* Even though I once screamed at her for letting my sister get her ears pierced before I did, and she slapped me across the face and stunned us both into silence, my mom and I are now great friends. We talk about mature subjects and enjoy a relationship that couldn't exist while I was a child.

This is more than possible for believers who are after maturity. "The LORD would speak to Moses face to face, as a man speaks with his friend" (Exodus 33:11).

At this point, how would you characterize your relationship with God? (A friendship? A parent-teen shouting match? Something else?)

2. *Graduating from the labors of constant discipline.* I can't wait to see the benefits of this training. One, I'd rather enjoy my kids. Two, if I'm not having to constantly discipline, it means it's working.

God trains us early to produce godliness later. At some point, we should graduate from constant discipline to consistent obedience. Hebrews 12:11 says, "No discipline seems pleasant at the time, but painful. Later on, however, it produces a harvest of righteousness and peace for those who have been trained by it." Where are you in this progression? (In the middle of painful discipline? Resting in the peace that comes after training? No idea?)

3. *Seeing my kids come into their own.* I can't wait to watch them develop their own gifts and grow in productivity so I can brag. Plus, I need to know they are capable enough to carry on my work when I'm old and crazy and have twelve cats.

God's not crazy, but He expects us to grow up into the gifts He gave each of us and do His work. A spiritual child is incapable of contributing. She neither knows her gifts nor has any inclination to impact God's kingdom.

What reasons, if any, have you given God in the last six months to brag on you?

4. *Securing our family's legacy.* Right now, my kids couldn't articulate the spiritual dynamics of our family, nor could they be expected to carry it forward. My Girlfriend Jen's son recently portrayed their roles in a pictorial (at school, of course): "My mom's job is to buy expensive things on the computer, and dad puts them in the barn and rides around on his tractor and yells at her." At age seven, that's the sum of who his parents are. I diligently pray my kids will one day allow *our* faith to become *their* faith and continue the legacy of a godly home for my grandkids and beyond.

From the beginning of time, God commissioned us to pass on His legacy as only mature believers can do. We cannot teach what we do not know. How are you doing with God's legacy in your home? Talk about what you think is and isn't working.

This is why God constantly urges His children to journey forward. Just as certainly as our physical bodies mature and grow as we age, our spiritual lives should also. It's a given. A nonnegotiable. It should be as obvious as the effects of gravity and ultraviolet rays.

But is it? If you are a believer, has your spiritual life progressed since you first stepped into faith? In what ways? In what ways has it not?

Would you honestly say you were *mostly* moving forward, holding steady, or falling backward?

Girls, if you've been held back, held up, or you're just trying to hold together, welcome to the Road Trip. Together, we will join forces with our patient Lord and begin the process of moving forward. Do you remember when I showed you the progress words that appeared so often in God's Word? Let me show you two more:

- run—71
- walk—133

Guess what? God values a steady pace almost two to one over a dash. Growing spiritually is a marathon, not a sprint. Just as I can't clap twice and transport my kids from elementary school to college graduation, spiritual maturity is a process that takes time. *A lifetime*. God wants to tuck you under His arm and gently put the car in drive. The road stretches ahead. Are you *willing* to go forward? That's all God needs from you to begin.

Psalm 143:8 in The Message says, "Point out the road I must travel; I'm all ears, all eyes before you." Girls, let's road trip.

Write a prayer to God. Offer Him your fears, reservations, willingness, and obedience. Include any Scripture or phrases that connected with you today.

DAY TWO

Road Narrows Ahead: Chart Your Course

When I turned sixteen, the time had come to put another unskilled teenage menace on the road who paid more attention to her driving vibe than to lesser considerations like other cars and yield signs. I figured I had earned the right to exercise the vibe because, purely by the intervention of God, I'd survived what is now referred to as "Dad's Driving School of Hard Knocks: A Horror."

Because my dad had poorly chosen to teach me to drive a *standard* during the Horror, two out of the following four things were happening every twenty feet: (1) I was killing the engine, (2) Dad was screaming, (3) gears were being ground down to a fine metal powder, or (4) I was bawling. It was pleasant. Only my brother got to escape the Horror, because by the time my parents survived three daughters, they were too tired to parent the baby.

This is the redeeming part: Dad had the wherewithal to teach me in the country on a little empty road. Granted, it appeared as if a crack addict and her psychotic companion were out for a joy ride, but there were no other dangers outside homicide or a spontaneous aneurysm. When I finally worked up the nerve to drive on the wide roads in town, I was so overwhelmed with my own potential for vehicular manslaughter, I had to pull over and call my rescuer: Dad.

He had chosen the right road to teach me on. It was smaller, had less distractions, fewer drivers. Frankly, it was the only safe place for a driver of my skill to maneuver. Of course, I wanted to drive in town and traverse the big city of Wichita. Everyone else did. I told him I could handle it, but Dad knew best.

The first step of any good trip is to *pick your road*. Where are you going? It seems like there are infinite possibilities. There is a road for every belief, desire, religion, and notion. Our world stamps these choices with tolerance and calls it "freedom." You call your own shots! There is no right or wrong because everything is relative! Pick your own road—it's your choice.

There are so many self-serving options, we can easily get lost. As He frequently did with laser-focused truth, Jesus boiled it all down to two roads. Read Matthew 7:13-14.

Let's take a close look at the narrow road. Verse 13 begins by saying, "Enter through the narrow gate." What is this? A gate for skinny people? What is God trying to do here? Cramp our style? Suffocate our personalities? Press down our dreams? Box us in? Why would we even want to pick this road?

First of all, Jesus is demonstrating His knack for showing the complex to be simple. This chapter marks what I call "the teaching of the twos." Jesus frequently taught like this: two sons, two debtors, two sowers, two slaves. Here's His point: It's simple. Choose one of two paths. We try to complicate matters and convince ourselves there is middle road, a merging. We invent intersections and connecting roads. We look at our spiritual journey in shades of gray.

Jesus tells us otherwise in Matthew 12:30: "He who is not with me is against me." Period. We are either after the things of Christ or we damage His name and set ourselves against Him. There is no middle road.

It begins at that narrow gate. This is the entrance, the start of the Road Trip. As Jesus kindly beckoned in Matthew 11:28, "Come to me, all you who are weary and burdened, and I will give you rest."

Why do you think Jesus placed a tiny gate at the entrance of the narrow road? Why didn't He frame the road with a huge, accommodating gate to make entering easier?

One thing I love about Jesus is that He was a realist. He never presented salvation as a rainbow-striped experience complete with fluffy white clouds and an unlimited supply of sour candy and full-calorie Dr. Pepper (no, wait, that's *my* heaven). No bait and switch here.

Read Luke 14:27-33. What is the point of Jesus' stories about the tower and the king?

Why do you think Jesus taught this? Why do we need to know this?

The small gate is the entrance from godlessness to salvation. Of all we've heard about God's miracles, here is the most astounding, unbelievable, incomprehensible miracle of them all. Jesus takes what was filthy and makes it perfect. He doesn't *pretend* to see us as clean or make merciful concessions for our faults. He washes us white as snow and replaces our sin with His righteousness.

Clearly we need to bend our proud necks to enter through this small gate, and it isn't until we're willing to lay face down before God in submission that we can truly fit through. We must throw off what has falsely inflated us. As we detach from worldly accolades that have puffed us up, *then* we are brought even lower. The void that was once filled with nothing but hot air is deflated, making room for God to fill us back up with His love.

If this sacrifice feels painful, may I lovingly tell you that we will either be brought low now of our own will or later at the hand of God? Jesus made it clear in Matthew 23:12: "For whoever exalts himself will be humbled, and whoever humbles himself will be exalted."

If you entered the way of salvation some time ago, how did you have to humble yourself, bend down, or lay something down in order to fit? If you're just now facing the gate for the first time, what do you find hardest to lay down?

The woman bowed low in worship can always fit through the gate. To recognize and adore God for who He is and what He has done can only leave us face down in praise.

With that, we face the narrow road. We've been granted entrance through Jesus, the Gatekeeper, and we move from the point of salvation to the business of living. To be sure, many believers have entered the gate and halted their journey five feet beyond the opening. But the Road Trip is a two-part engagement. The Gatekeeper tipped us off in Matthew: "But small is the *gate* and narrow the *road* that leads to life, and only a few find it" (7:14).

*Just as He commissioned a narrow gate, Jesus sets us on a narrow road. List every reason you can think of as to why the road to maturity is described as narrow.

The word *narrow* is from the Greek word *thlibo* meaning "a compressed way; narrow straightened; contracted." The best way to understand the necessity of the narrow road is to compare it to the wide road.

The other road is "broad," with plenty of room for every godless theory, each selfish ambition, any mix of beliefs, and all demonstrations of greed, lust, and pride. This path offers its travelers many liberties. There is no accountability, boundaries, or regulations. You are welcome to run straight into the arms of any sin of your choosing. You'll be hedged in by nothing.

From this perspective of the broad road, why is the narrow road defined as "a compressed way"?

Because the broad road has so many options, it frequently splits, twists, drops off, runs into itself, and contains dangerous intersections. Matthew Henry said, "*A broad way*, for there are many paths in it; there is choice of sinful ways, *contrary to each other*, but all paths in this broad way."[2] Two opposite yet powerful sins often collide violently. Selfish paths intersect to the ruin of one or both travelers. There is no system, no engineering, no standard road rules.

Considering the other travelers, why might the narrow road be defined as "straightened"?

Both destinations are twofold. The wide road is alluring. Most are enticed to casually walk through that enormous gate where their wildest dreams await them, but it's a lure. They will only and always find destruction there, both during this life and after. Because guess what? Turns out that road is lonely, crowded yet empty, dangerous, and ultimately a dead end. For *every* traveler. Destruction now. Eternal destruction later. It is, most certainly, a bait and switch.

But Girls, the narrow road leads to life! Real life now. Eternal life later. Jesus told us to count the cost before we choose Him, but the rewards are riches beyond measure. This is what awaits us on the narrow road, hedged in by godly boundaries for our protection. For every sacrifice we make, every border we stay within, and every inch we bow lower before our God, it is returned to us a hundredfold in fellowship with the Creator, forgiveness, and blessings outside of the realm of our wildest dreams.

But that is not why we choose this path. We choose it because our dearest Friend, our most tender Jesus, stands at the entrance and says, "Come to Me. I know you're tired and weary. I love you more than you'll ever understand, and I want to give you rest. Precious daughter, let's journey together."

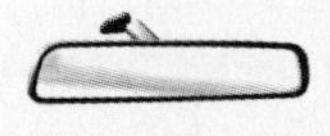

*Where are you? (Outside the gate? Through the gate but standing still? Traveling forward?)

Are you ready to head down the narrow road? Write a prayer to Jesus either thanking Him for His companionship on this road you're already on, or asking Him to journey with you as you begin the ultimate Road Trip. Offer Him your commitment to begin moving forward.

DAY THREE

Dumping Grounds: Travel Light

I got a phone call from my Girlfriend Trina recently. I picked up the phone and knew right away something was wrong:

Jen: Hello?
Trina: Jen, it's me. I'm in trouble.
Jen: What's wrong? What happened?!
Trina: I'm shopping for clothes, and all of a sudden, *(whispering)* I don't know what I'm supposed to wear anymore! I'm looking at an outfit thinking, "That's cute. My sister would wear that," but she's twenty years older than me!
Jen: Calm down. I'm sure it's not that bad. Is the waistband elastic? Does it have matching embroidery around the sleeves and cuffs?
Trina: HOW DID YOU KNOW?! And it gets worse . . .
Jen: Please tell me you did not buy suntan pantyhose.
Trina: I'm holding a pair of skorts.

Jen: *(gasp)* Trina, listen very carefully to me. Put the skorts down and back away slowly. Back away! Look for the nearest exit!

Trina: But it's a skirt that acts like shorts.

Jen: Stop it!! You're scaring me! It starts with one pair of skorts, and you think you can handle them. You think you can. But the next thing you know, you're wearing Easy Spirits and eating dinner at 4:00! This is so dangerous! That's it. Don't try to get yourself out of this. I'm coming right now. Just sit down on the floor and wait for me.

I found her in the "Active Woman" department at Penney's, and I barely got her out in time. I'll be honest, it was a near miss. I almost lost her.

Jen *(being gentle yet firm)*: What happened in there?

Trina: I don't know. I just got so confused. *(wailing)* So distracted! There were too many coordinates! I was surrounded! All I could see were embroidered butterflies and cardigans!

Jen: Oh, Trina! You must have been so scared!

Trina: Don't ever let me shop alone again. I get sensory overload and feel the need to dress like my mother.

Jen: Repeat after me: "Clean lines, flattering cuts, solids not patterns, basics. Basics! Simple styles! If you want to be a sparkly pants, it must be confined to your accessories. Do you understand?

Trina: This is going into the "hilarious category," isn't it? You're going to write about this, aren't you?

Jen *(patting Trina gently)*: Of course I am.

Overload. It can get the best of us. It is so much more difficult, if not downright impossible, to move forward when we're weighed down. Preoccupations can quickly turn the Road Trip of a Lifetime into drudgery. It's easy to become distracted by worries, guilt, shame, sin, anxiety, busy-ness, you name it. Girls, this is a long trip, and we must pack well. Jesus has made it abundantly clear how to go about it: "Stay simple. Travel light." Where we tend to add layers, responsibilities, and clutter, Jesus takes the opposite approach.

Jesus said, "Blessed are the pure in heart, for they will see God" (Matthew 5:8). What do you think He meant by "pure in heart"?

This word *pure* is from the Greek word *katharos*. It is used twenty-two times in the New Testament. It carries three separate but cohesive meanings, all under the definition of "clean." I can hear Jesus urging, *begging us* to simplify.

- *katharos*: clean ethically; free from corrupt desire, from sin and guilt

Here's the truth: You can't really travel this road when you're loaded down with sin. You may carry so much sinful baggage, you've literally come to a screeching halt. Or you may manage to move slowly, but carrying your sin is like pulling a trailer. Everyone is passing you, and the slightest breeze sends you all over the road. Either way, Jesus wants you to feel the wind in your hair, and sin can only hinder your progress. This includes sin in action, motive, or thought.

*Read Psalm 32:1-4. Have you ever felt like David? What was it like?

Are you carrying sin that needs to be confessed? If so, what is it?

And did you catch that last part of the definition? "Clean from sin and *guilt*." Is it possible to be cleansed from sin but still carry its guilt? Can you go on a diet and not lose one pound? Of course it's possible, and it happens all the time. Have you ever asked God to forgive something He has already forgiven? You know you have. That's guilt talking, Girls. Since the Enemy can't deny us forgiveness from a holy God, he'll try to deny us its freedom. Through guilt, he presses us down with his lies:

"They don't know the real you."
"You'll never change."
"No one else struggles like you."
"You can't escape it."
"You may be forgiven, but God is still disappointed."

This is where our Hero enters. Jesus, through His loving sacrifice, took our sin with its nasty guilt, nailed it on the cross, and conquered it when He rose again. Did you see what His purity, His *katharos*, looks like? Not just unstained from sin, but *unstained from guilt*. Jesus holds us close and says, "You're forgiven. You're clean. You're pure. Completely."

Go back to David's passage in Psalm 32 and read verses 5-7. How does David sound different in this section than in verses 3-4?

Is there anything more we could ask for? We can choose to travel a lifetime dragging our guilt behind us, slowing our journey, making it painful when it should be joyful—and it's just that: a choice. But Jesus allows us to throw it off with abandon by commanding us, "Do not call anything impure that God has made clean" (Acts 10:15).

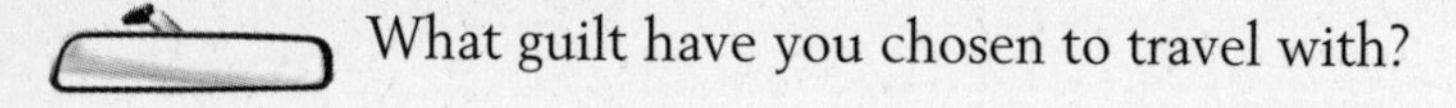

What guilt have you chosen to travel with?

What keeps you from leaving it behind? Are you willing to?

And while we're busy cleaning out, let's go to one more place. I'm a fan of this next one. Any of my friends would testify to this fact: Jen Hatmaker saves nothing. If it is not a breathing member of this family or doesn't possess alarming levels of sentiment, it's trash fodder. I figure it's less that my kids will have to give away to Salvation Army after I kick off. While I know the pack rats judge me for having no detectable soul, I also have no detectable clutter. Take that.

So speaking of clutter, let's talk about cleaning out our schedules. Uh oh. Here we go. Let's read this cute little piece Paul wrote to Timothy as he described an approved workman for God.

Read 2 Timothy 2:20-21. What point do you think Paul is making here?

I know in the weekly schedule I've chosen, I have some gold and silver investments. These select responsibilities enrich my family life or advance kingdom work, no exceptions. But wood and clay opportunities constantly tempt my boundaries. Sign up for this; help lead that; put your kids in this; take on that. Not that they are bad things (what's not to love about KinderGym?), but they would serve ignoble purposes in my life and the life of my family.

*According to verse 21, how do you think wood and clay time investments ultimately serve ignoble purposes?

Let me tell you something: If you don't become the PTA Treasurer, it doesn't mean your kids will get the bad teachers who hate children. If your son doesn't start T-ball by the time he's four, who cares? He's not going to the Majors, and that college scholarship your husband keeps referencing is a crapshoot, too. These things aren't bad, but string too many of them together, and they become wood and clay in your life.

"If a man cleanses himself from the latter, he will be an instrument for noble purposes, made holy, useful to the Master and prepared to do any good work."

What have you committed to (or committed your kids to) that is serving ignoble purposes either by overextending or distracting you?

What gold and silver commitments should you boil your schedule down to?

Blessed are the pure in heart, for they will see God" (Matthew 5:8). This is what Jesus was talking about. Pure. Simple. Basic. Clean. We are not governed by our sin, oppressed with our shame, or dictated by our schedules. Though it makes us uncomfortable and vulnerable to empty out, we cannot enjoy the Road Trip until we're light enough to move forward.

The world says, "Take the wide road, and pack all your comforts."

Jesus says, "Take the narrow road, and unpack everything you've so carefully arranged. Leave plenty of trunk space for our journey. You have no idea how I'm going to fill it up."

Take some time to journal to God. Consider these three areas of purity, and what needs to be accomplished in your life for each one. Ask Him to show you any areas you missed and to give you strength to throw off the weight that slows you down.

DAY FOUR

HOV Lane: Travel Together

I'm a terrible driver when I'm alone. It always seems like a great idea at first. I relish the notion of being in the car without the following verbal barrage assaulting me like tiny, individual daggers stabbing away at the thin flesh of my sanity:

"Mommy? Do you know how to teleport?"
"Mommy? How many seconds have you been alive?"
"Mommy? What's five billion times ten million?"
"Mommy? When I go to college, will you be dead?"
"Mommy? Why are you talking so angry?"

But the reality of driving alone is much different than in beautiful, peaceful theory. I get bored. I get tired. With my arm on the steering wheel, I notice how loose the flesh is under my arm as it hangs like a slab of beef. I obsess about this slab by repeatedly pinching it with my free hand. I promise the slab I will take it to the gym and attempt to eradicate it. I drift off the shoulder of the road and am scared into attentiveness for at least four minutes. I flip through the radio stations and discover I don't know who is popular anymore—*and I was cool just a few years ago*. Land sakes! Am I there yet? How much longer?

I should have brought a friend.

Traveling alone just doesn't compare to traveling with friends. Friends take turns driving. They justify your road food choices. They tell funny stories until one friend has to pull over and potty in the grass. They bring their cool music so you don't have to listen to your Gavin DeGraw CD for the ten-millionth time. They let you read articles out loud to them without rolling their eyes. They make the trip *so much better*.

Paul says, "You were all called to travel on the same road and in the same direction, so stay together, both outwardly and inwardly" (Ephesians 4:4, MSG). For believers, there is but one road. I'm on it. You're on it. It's so narrow that we can't help but touch each other. Let's travel together.

God told us from the beginning of time how He felt about our journey. "It is not good for. . . man to be alone" (Genesis 2:18).

*On your *spiritual* journey, are you traveling with friends, or are you mainly driving alone? Why?

This is not a gray area. The wisest man in the history of God's Word gave us some strong reasons to travel together. What did Solomon teach us about the value of godly friendship in the following verses?

Proverbs 15:22

Proverbs 17:17

Proverbs 27:9

Ecclesiastes 4:9-10

What do the above verses tell you about God?

Paul describes the foundation of authentic community in Philippians 2:1-4. What picture of unity do you see in verse 1?

Unity is central to God's magnificence. God the Father, the beloved Son, and the Holy Spirit represent the epitome of unity. Three in one: the perfect display of togetherness. They model for us how to defer in honor of another:

- Jesus "did not consider equality with God something to be grasped, but made himself nothing" (Philippians 2:6-7). Humility.
- In response, "God exalted him to the highest place and gave him the name that is above every name" (Philippians 2:9). Glory deferred to another.
- Jesus prioritized our need for the Spirit over His own life: "It is for your good that I am going away. Unless I go away, the Counselor will not come to you; but if I go, I will send him to you" (John 16:7). Best interests of others.

All for one and one for all if I ever saw it. What would their unity have looked like if Jesus had decided in the garden that God's will should take a back seat to His own well-being? What if God became jealous of the glory due Jesus and left Him in the grave? What if the Spirit decided He was sick of dispensing God's wisdom all the time? Their unity is the salvation we relish, the guidance we starve for. The happiness and goodness of the entire world is founded on sacrificial unity.

So it stands to reason that God and Jesus and the Spirit would want this togetherness, this divine love for their followers—not only directed toward their divinity, but toward other believers. Imagine the goodness God could harness out of our obedient unity.

Paul described this unity in Philippians 2:2-4. List as many benefits you can think of to living like this.

*What seem to be the greatest enemies of Christian unity?

It's easy to travel together as mothers. We have so much in common. We naturally travel together as women. We understand each other. We can journey through careers, marriage, recreation, and hobbies quite casually. I can talk with a perfect stranger for two hours simply on the distinctions of "Breasts: Pre- versus Post-Kids." But genuinely traveling together as *believers* is a path less taken, even among those who believe.

Why is that? For me, pride whispers, "Don't let them know you struggle." "You must only have answers, not questions." "Leaders should never divulge their own sins." "You cannot show yourself weak." What will they think? What will they say? Who will I be if I'm not who they think I am? The trip together becomes inauthentic, and an atmosphere of falsehood drifts in.

Fear is simply the flip side of pride. Fear often takes root after being burned by another Christian, well-intentioned or not. You swore you'd never be close to those flames again. It sometimes comes from the other side of the experience tracks. You're scared to display your lack of knowledge. You hesitate to voice your questions. They seem immature or sacrilegious. You fear the vulnerability, the proximity. You're scared to invite the observations of others. You're reluctant to show where you've come from or where you really are.

*What enemy of unity do you struggle with? How has it affected your spiritual journey?

Is there a specific step you need to take? Get real with other Christians? Restore unity with another believer?

Now does this mean we have to sit in circles and hold hands and chant every time we get together? That's entirely optional, but I'd suggest that a holy friendship is actually much simpler. In her book *Traveling Together*, Karla Worley says:

As we travel together toward our goal of full maturity, we are joined at the hip. One slows down for the other, carries the other, encourages the other, depends on the other. Each challenges, paces, corrects, spurs the other toward the goal. My function as your friend in Christ is to equip you to walk toward the goal. The question I must ask is: As your friend, how can I help you become more like Christ? In everything we do together—play, work, endure, enjoy, hope, plan, dream, celebrate—in every moment of our friendship, this is my role."[3]

Oh, do I know this celebration of friendship! Outside God and my family, there is not a group that gives me happiness and carries me forward more than my Girlfriends. They give me a part in holy unity, godly togetherness. My Girlfriend Stevie was doing long-term mission work in Mexico when another worker saw a picture of our circle of friends. She asked Stevie, "Are these your sisters?" Stevie smiled and nodded, "Yes indeed. Those are my sisters."

Do you have godly friends to celebrate? If not, would you risk inviting a travel companion or two to journey forward with you? Who will you ask?

Oh, Girls, if you have ever known encouragement from Jesus during your darkest moment, evidence that by strengthening your sisters in Christ. If He has ever united with your broken spirit, respond in turn by linking arms with each other. If you have felt the warm embrace of comfort from the Spirit, liberally deliver that same nourishment. If fellowship with the Creator has ever made you shout out loud, try on the celebration of Girlfriends. If the tenderness of Jesus has ever brought you to your knees, choose forgiveness over retaliation. If compassion from heaven has ever left you breathless, give it away with the same generosity.

That's joy completed.

This begins with you. There is no place on this narrow road for carefully constructed walls or façades. You may keep them, but you'll never know the joy, the celebration, the holiness of friendship in God's world. It's time to hold your hands out and say, "This is the real me. These are my real struggles. I'll love the real you, if you'll love the real me." You have no idea how much your trip will change when you invite travel companions to journey with you on the narrow road.

Is your car full of people cheering you on to godliness? Do you wish it was? Ask God to show you what you need to change to accommodate authentic friendships. Ask for specific friends, and be willing to let them in.

If you know the joy of godly friends, ask God if you need to *be* a friend to a lonely traveler.

DAY FIVE

Rest Stop

On the last day of each week, you will have the opportunity to spend some focused time in prayer and journaling. Please do not skip this. This can mark a day when what has filled your mind can infect your heart and supply your worship.

Remember God's words in 1 Samuel 16:7: "Man looks at the outward appearance, but the LORD looks at the heart." Filled in blanks and answered questions mean nothing to God if they don't draw you closer to Him. *Nothing*. He never asked for a completed workbook. He has only asked for your heart. If the first doesn't lead to the second, it is a complete waste of time. Give Him your undivided attention today.

Turn to Psalm 23. Use the following guide to lead you through this Scripture. You may use the prompts provided or allow the Spirit to lead you differently. Spend a few minutes on each verse in prayer. Feel free to jot down your thoughts in your journal as you go.

- Read Psalm 23:1: Spend a few minutes in prayer acknowledging your Shepherd. Are you one of His own? Do you know Him? Thank Him for guarding you, saving you, protecting you, loving you, *knowing you*. The Lord is *my* shepherd.

- Read Psalm 23:2: Does your life feel still and quiet? Does your schedule conflict with God's peace? Offer up any distractions or over-commitments that keep you from God's business. Ask Him to show you what is not a necessity but a distraction.
- Read Psalm 23:3: Have you been restored? Do you know the forgiveness and mercy of Jesus? Or are you still dragging around your shame? Praise Him for His restoring hands. Only God can make you better than new.
- Read Psalm 23:3 again: Are you on this path of righteousness for His name's sake? Thank Him for allowing you to walk this road. Praise Him for the boundaries with which He has hedged you in. Declare them protective, not restrictive.
- Read Psalm 23:4: Will you choose to walk forward, no matter what you encounter on the path? Are you willing to journey even if it moves you to the uncomfortable, even the painful? Ask God to strengthen you for progress. Ask Him to help you put one foot in front of the other and move.
- Read Psalm 23:5: This table David writes of symbolized a meal shared after making a covenant together. It expressed the bond of friendship. How is your table? Full? Empty? Praise God for the friends He has given you for this journey. Name them individually. Or ask God to supply your table with companions and be willing to invite them in.
- Read Psalm 23:6: The woman moving forward is followed constantly by her sidekicks: goodness and mercy. We don't travel alone. Thank God for His goodness specifically. How has He simply been a good God to you? Praise Him for His mercy. Ask for an extra measure as you travel forward and encounter five major areas of growth. He is patient with the pure hearted.

Take some time to journal. Include your thoughts, questions, fears, thanksgivings, and commitments. Thoroughly explore your responses to this week's work. If you've thrown off some hindrances this week, list them. Be honest. Close your journal time with a written prayer offering your transparency and truthfulness to God.

WEEK TWO

Identity

(Samaritan Woman at the Well)

DAY ONE

Road Block One: Culture

My daughter, Sydney, asked me the other day, "Mommy? What's the easiest job there is? I'm trying to figure out who I'm gonna be when I grow up, and I don't want to work hard." *There's* that work ethic we'd been trying to instill. Kind of makes a mom want to cry and pray her daughter isn't living on her couch at age twenty-eight because "things just don't work out for her." I asked her what she thought the easiest job was (as an easy job is better than no job).

"Probably a doctor. You just look in ears and tell people to take medicine." Can't fault her logic there. I asked her if she wanted to be a doctor, then.

Big sighs and dramatic head rolling. "No! I want to be the hardest job of all: a cheerleader! But you have to do all those tricks!" Alas, a dream thwarted by the challenges of tumbling. She'll have to settle for neurology or basic endocrinology. She'll tell her patients: "I had big dreams once. But not everyone can flip."

At age five, my underachiever is already thinking about who she'll one day be. She talks of a career (a loose term), being a wife, a mom. At this earliest stage, she is already searching for value. Will I be important? Will I matter? Who will I be? Who will others say I am? These are the basic questions we carry to the grave. The most spiritually healthy women on the planet have traveled this path well: the road trip of Identity.

This week, we're going to walk with a woman who courageously threw off what had poorly defined her in exchange for an identity that would revolutionize not only her own life, but her entire people.

Read John 4:1-5. Look at the map on page 47 and notice the geography of Jesus' journey: Jesus left from _______, and He traveled north through _______ on his way to _______.

Five minutes of history, if you'll allow me (this *really* informs the story, so focus for just a smidge). Although those verses seem unremarkable, they are wholly relevant. Judea (a province in the southern Holy Land, with its capital in Jerusalem) had terrible relations with her neighbor to the north, Samaria. The rift began seven hundred years earlier when Samaria (once the capital of the northern kingdom of Israel back when they were all friends) was captured by Assyria.

Back then, an Assyrian governor was set over Samaria, and some 28,000 Samaritans were deported and replaced with various people from eastern cultures. These "new Samaritans" brought their religions and their gods. The monotheistic worship of God was polluted.

Not good. It pretty much spiraled down from there. The "new Samaritans" regained their independence about a hundred years later and adopted the first five books of the Bible (the Pentateuch or Torah) from the Jews. They gave it a Samaritan alphabetic twist and promptly rejected the remainder of the Hebrew Bible.

What's more, they taunted the Jews by saying their version of the Torah was older and they observed its precepts better. Tell a Jewish Pharisee you obey the Law better than he does, and be ready to duck. Especially when he thinks you're a big, fat pagan descended from mixed, idolatrous races that ignore most of the

Hebrew Bible and worship in a runner-up temple on Mount Gerizim (in Samaria) rather than the real temple in Jerusalem.

This strife trickled down into Jesus' day. The Jews rejected the Samaritan version of the Torah, detested their defective devotion to Judaism, and publicly cursed them in their synagogues. Samaritans couldn't serve as witnesses in Jewish courts, they could *not* be converted to Judaism, even if they wanted to be, and according to the Jews, they were excluded from the afterlife.

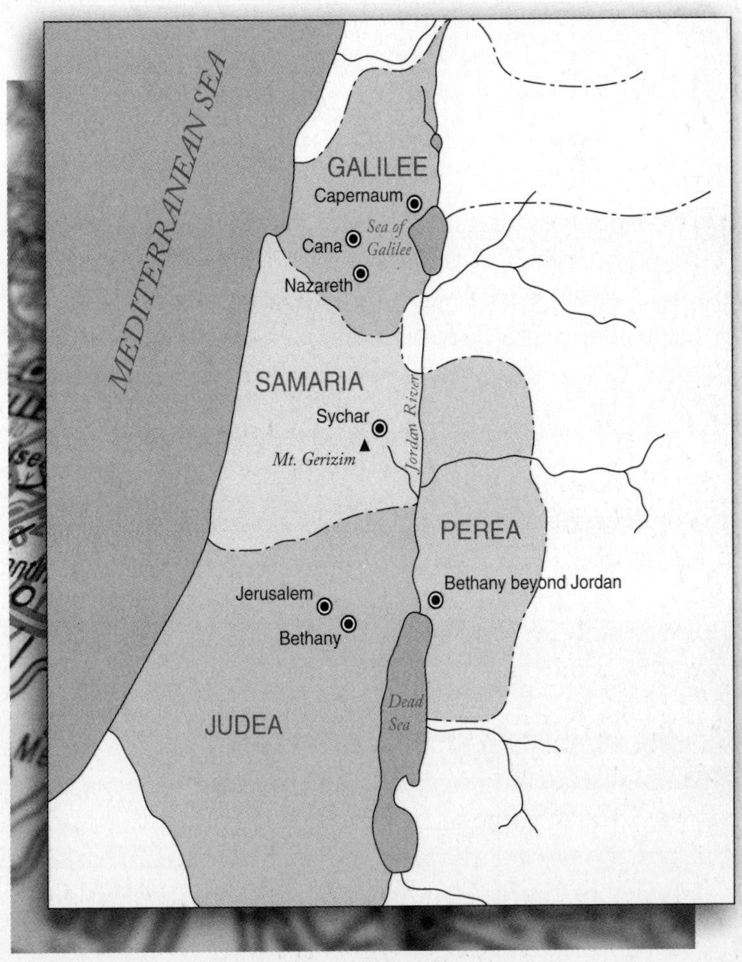

Jesus' Journey Through Samaria

How would you summarize what the Jews thought of Samaritans? What were their deepest emotions?

Given their history, how do you think the Samaritans felt about the Jews? Why?

So in John 4:4 when Jesus "had to go through Samaria," there's one more thing to understand. While yes, Samaria lay squarely between Judea in the south and Galilee in the north, most Jews would cross to the eastern side of the Jordan River rather than pass through Samaria, where they believed they could be contaminated simply by proximity.[1] But here we see Jesus leading His disciples straight through Samaria on their seventy-mile walk to Galilee.

*What does this tell you about the kind of man Jesus was?

Read John 4:6-9. Why do you think Jesus asked this woman to give Him a drink?

We can safely say there was a culture clash here. Jesus represented all that was true and real. As He stood there—fully man, thirsty and tired—He was also fully God. All the wrong ways stood in stark contrast to the Only Way, embodied here in the gentle, risky behavior of the Son of God.

On the other hand, this woman was a product of Samaria. Her heritage had given her a distorted faith, a partial knowledge. It pressed its ideals on her, forming her identity and shaping her beliefs. Yet as she stood there, she probably assumed the Samaritan way was the right way.

Look at John 4:9,12,20. Where do you see Samaritan culture influencing her identity?

Our country has an inescapable identity, too. We are assaulted by images and suggestions on what to believe and who to be. We most certainly belong to the "American Way." Any attention to what the rest of the world says about our culture brings it into stark relief. Sometimes in a positive way, sometimes in a negative way, we hear: "They've been Americanized."

*List as many characteristics of American culture as you can think of. (Examples: Fast food, consumer goods, democracy.)

It's hard to think about, isn't it? For most of us, the American way seems like the only way, the right way, or, if we're truthful, the best way. This illustrates the underlying core value of our culture: individualism. We are wholly concerned with the advancement of the individual: her progress, her freedoms, her self-entitlement, her rights, her wardrobe. The customs of other cultures that value extended family and cohesive group systems over the individual ring oppressive and suffocating to Americans. Families having a say in who a girl marries? Please! We obviously know how to pick a lifelong mate on our own. Check our statistics. Where other cultures stress group identification and cooperation, we stress independence, self-reliance, and personal choice.[2]

*How do some of the values of our culture negatively affect the way we follow Jesus?

What biblical principles can you think of that fly in the face of American culture?

Americans are not ultimately so different from Samaritans. We've built our culture on selected parts of the Bible, not the whole thing. In doing so, we've settled for a distorted worldview, accepted lies over truth, and adopted the American identity as our standard. We've embraced a partial faith, enough to make us feel like a "good person" or hopefully advance our agendas, but certainly not the whole kit and caboodle. That's for the zealots. Our partial faith feels familiar, appropriate even, until we hold it up to the authenticity of Jesus. Then it's revealed as oppressive, false, a road to nowhere paved with insecurity. That's not to say America is worse than anywhere else—*every* culture is a Samaria compared to the kingdom of God.

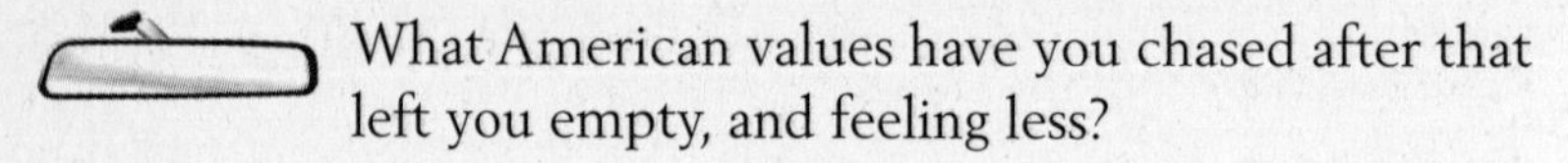

What American values have you chased after that left you empty, and feeling less?

This journey of identity begins with Jesus at that well. He will challenge our definition of self. He'll take away what falsely defines us and replace it with what is real. The American standards we wrap ourselves in will be stripped away, leaving us temporarily bare. It's a revolutionary journey, but it's not optional. No healthy believer can move forward with a false sense of self. That cuts the legs out from underneath progress.

Identity is anchored not in who we are, but in who Jesus is. The American image depends solely on *our* efforts, *our* merits, *our* presentation of self. But Girls, our true identity is completely blanketed, duct-taped, bubble-wrapped, and packaged in the person of Jesus. Any understanding of the individual outside of Him is irrelevant. Let's discover the radical, revolutionary gift of identity graciously given by Jesus at that sweet well.

Is your identity you-centered or Jesus-centered? Have you latched on to any empty ideals? Ask God to prepare you for truth this week.

DAY TWO

Road Block Two: Gender

I'm not a raging, angry feminist sporting an offensive she-mullet. I don't think all men are chauvinist women-haters just trying to keep a sister down. I don't feel like "the man" has held me back (although I'd like to meet the man who could rein in this wild filly). I think most men are good people who view women with respect and just a teensy bit of fear, bless their hearts.

I'm telling you this because we're taking a look today at how *some* men have falsely defined many women. Sadly, it's a tale as old as time. The Enemy keeps recycling this identity-crusher with each new era. It takes on different forms and boundaries, but the result is the same.

Let's begin with our forerunner, the Samaritan woman. Read John 4:7-9 again. Can you hear the shock in her voice? We've already discovered the opposing cultures of Judea and Samaria. That was reason enough for this conversation never to happen. But the addition of her gender sends this right over the edge into scandalous.

This is a familiar story, and you've probably heard how Jesus talking to a woman was radical, but let me deepen your understanding of this social train wreck. Here are just a few adorable facts about women in first-century Judea and surrounding areas:

- According to rabbinic literature, women were not to be acknowledged or spoken to in the street—not even a man to his own wife. In fact, a woman was to walk six paces behind her husband.
- Men could "dismiss" their wives in divorce for any reason they deemed offensive, from adultery to burning their dinner (true!). Women had no divorce rights.
- Women could play no role in the synagogue and received precious little religious education.
- Women could not be disciples of any great rabbi and certainly couldn't travel with one.
- Men had complete authority over women in establishing their activities and relationships. A father ruled his daughter until he passed her to a husband of his choosing.[3]
- Women couldn't recite the daily prayers or read the Torah, and they weren't required to come to any religious feasts or festivals.[4] In fact, first-century Rabbi Eliezer declared, "Rather should the words of the Torah be burned than entrusted to a woman."[5] Nice. He and I wouldn't have gotten along.

Given these fun little facts, list five words to describe how you think first-century women in these parts saw themselves.

So here we have a male Jewish rabbi talking to a Samaritan woman (with a disgraceful history, but we'll get there later) in broad daylight. This was madness! Insanity! To lower himself to talk to a woman, this rabbi must have been desperate for water. He still probably thought she was scum. Yet there was something gentle in his voice and fire in his eyes when he asked her for something to drink.

*What does our culture tell women to be like? Specifically, what identity markers are encouraged for your stage in life—single, young wife, mother, empty-nester? (Examples: Beautiful, sexy, maternal, graceful, in control.)

After her understandable response, Jesus launched right into grace. A connection was made. Chitchat was over.

Read John 4:10-13. What do you think Jesus meant by "living water"?

*By choosing terms like "living water" and "never thirst," what did Jesus seem to know about the state of her soul?

I love Jesus. He graciously eased her into truth. To me, the most important thing Jesus established here is that if she knew what to ask for, *He would give it to her* (verse 10). He knew she wouldn't understand yet, but He was breaking down barriers that had poorly defined her. He would bless her, not diminish her. It was a tall order.

For her—and for us—it's often a hardship to calculate our identity outside the men who have defined us. It becomes ingrained, accepted as fact. For more women than I can number, that identification began a long time ago: as little girls growing up in our father's house.

Sweet Girls, how have you defined yourself—positively or negatively—as a result of your relationship with your father?

We don't know about the Samaritan woman's childhood, but I'll bet she never dreamed about the reality she experienced as an adult. Mutuality was a concept Jesus introduced, but she'd likely never experienced it. Although we'll explore it in detail tomorrow, verse 18 tells us she had been divorced five times. And as we studied earlier, only men could instigate divorce at this time.

What might the Samaritan woman have believed about herself at this point in her life?

This is why we see her at the well at high noon in the heat of the day (verse 6), though the other women came in the evening when it was cooler. She'd come here alone in her brokenness, spared from further humiliation by human contact.

Have you known pain from a man (or men) that has affected your identity? If so, describe your circumstance.

Satan capitalizes on the shortcomings of mankind. He takes the mistakes, poor decisions, the sins of men against women, and uses them to make matters worse. In your vulnerability, he whispers lies capable of transforming a wound into an identity:

"You deserved this."
"You brought this on yourself."
"You were unworthy of his love."
"You were unworthy."
"You are unworthy."

*What identity, if any, did you adopt to manage the reality that was handed to you?

Dearest Girls, can you hear Jesus instead? "If you really knew who I was, you would ask *Me* for what is real, what is lasting, and *I would give it to you*. You are worthy of the gift." He doesn't look at you through human eyes of disrespect. Jesus doesn't see you as damaged, irrelevant. He won't turn His back on you and leave you devastated and alone.

He knows how you've been falsely defined, just as He knew how the Samaritan woman had been. Jesus also understands that when we seek worth from humanity, specifically men, we'll never be satisfied. Even in good relationships, we will be let down. We'll know betrayal, abuse, neglect, disappointment. It will never be enough.

What do you think Jesus wanted her (and us) to understand in verses 13-14?

Listen, you may be in the small but fortunate category: those that have only known men who've loved and respected them. I was passed from the kindest hands of my dad to the loving hands of my husband. The important men in my life have given me much value. You may have a similar story, but even *that* history is a dim reflection of the worth that comes from Jesus. The goal of our journey to identity is not to discover who we are in our own estimation or in the opinions of others. The goal is to discover who we are in Jesus. No human can replicate that value.

Simple but not easy, I know. It begins with a conscious choice to look away from the eyes of mankind into Jesus' eyes instead, and discover compassion. Find His strong gaze of esteem. Believe that Jesus is radically pro-woman. He sees you as the woman you are: His. He isn't influenced by what other men have said or concluded. Their opinions are a nonfactor. There is you, and there is Him, and out of the two of you, He is enough.

According to this exchange so far, how would you say Jesus felt about the Samaritan woman, damaged identity and all?

If Jesus could transform the Samaritan woman—who had the very tidal waves of culture against her—then He can change you. He looks at you with the same compassion that engaged the Samaritan woman at the well. She gave us a clue on how to begin: "Where can you get this living water?" she asked simply, and the journey began.

Friends, Jesus is the only man worthy of defining you. Where there was once shame, He brings honor. Humiliation gives way to value that is purely supernatural. You can't even imagine it until you've surrendered to it. Jesus' fierce gaze holds you close as He takes your face in His sweet hands, and says, "You belong to Me."

Will you bravely ask how to get this living water that can change who you are? Choose today who you will find value from. You cannot know your identity in Jesus while begging for worth from mankind. Ask God to shift your gaze to Jesus and be ready to see yourself in a whole new light.

DAY THREE

Road Block Three: Sin

I have some traits that were stamped into my DNA, pure and simple. For example, my entire family has two volumes: sleeping and loud. Every last one of us also has an impressive capacity for melodrama. It's genetic. What's worse, because of my birth order (first), the entire world is a black-and-white place for me. Things are right, and things are wrong. The end. The gray areas are only for the middle children and the rebellious babies.

Other qualities, I take full blame for. For instance, I have a little problem called "I hate most other drivers." It manifests as road rage. I'm not proud, I'm just saying I own it. I also have a little bit of a sassy mouth. I mean to be kind and precious all the time, but I get annoyed. And sometimes when I plan on being Mom Extraordinaire, I accidentally vaporize what little patience I have and several people end up crying. These things are mine. They are a teeny cross-section of what my husband dubs "my problem areas."

We all have some environmental factors to consider, the ones we were born into. These factors defined us early on. We came to understand them as "the way things are." We were handed these by our culture, our families, the men we've known. A certain reality was crafted for us, and in it, we adopted a specific identity to manage it. As we've studied, this takes on many shapes:

"Be perfect or act like you are."
"Appearance is everything."
"You will amount to nothing."
"Men cheat."
"Sex is your only card."
"Abandonment is inevitable."

Our American culture combined with our personal culture have messed up most women I know. We are given these "truths" and have little ability to separate ourselves from their message. Fortunately, Jesus has eradicated the missteps of mankind through His perfect gift. He has cast off the images of the world in favor of the namesake of His Father.

But there is another set of considerations that we must plow through in order to settle into the perfect identity Christ offers: the identity we've crafted through our own sin. We have to own this. The Samaritan woman certainly had been given a set of inadequacies to work with: You're a Samaritan—much less than a Judean. You're a woman—much less than a man. But to this she added her own sin, creating an identity we can bet she never dreamed of as a little girl.

Read John 4:15. After Jesus spoke of the living water He'd gladly give her, what did she demonstrate about herself through her response?

Read John 4:16-18. If this woman lived in our day, how would you probably describe her? Be honest.

She'd been "dismissed" five times, and she wasn't married to her newest lover. Although women could be divorced easily, this was highly unusual even for her times. Something had gone awry. In five divorces, the only common denominator was her. Adultery? We don't know, but she was currently sleeping with a man she wasn't married to, so we know sexual immorality was a familiar path.

This was her Achilles' heel, her sinful identity. It might have begun as a singular heartache but progressed as an image she wrapped herself in. She was the Sexual Vixen. If you can't beat 'em, join 'em. Though it originated in pain, her image was now something familiar. Something even embraced.

*Do you have an identity rooted in sin? Party girl? Man-hater? Miss Perfect? Martyr? Control Freak? Maybe something more subtle? Dig deep.

Why do you think Jesus said what He did in verse 16?

We cannot skip this. This may be the sweetest demonstration of Jesus' mercy in this whole story. He obviously knew her completely. He knew how she'd wielded her sexuality as her one bargaining chip. The Jesus many of us have created would have said, "Girl, get it together! You are a mess! Keep your pants on! Straighten up!" He would have rebuked and admonished her with a scathing account of her promiscuous life.

This is what we often expect when coming to Jesus in our sin. We anticipate judgment, horror, shock on His part. We steel ourselves for a liberal dousing of "shame on you." At best, we try to avert our eyes from the disappointed shake of Jesus' head as He is forced to deal with our sin.

*What do you expect to hear from Jesus when faced with *your* sin?

What does His attitude seem to be in verses 16-18 toward this sinful woman? Condemnation? Permissiveness? Indifference? What do you see?

"What you have just said is quite true." And Jesus stopped talking. Oh my land! Who is this guy? What an exchange! I could hover here for a year. I can feel the tension crackling in the air. Everyone had a choice here: Jesus in His manner of confrontation, the Samaritan woman in her response. She didn't sign up for this noon encounter, but Jesus certainly had a goal. After all, "he *had* to go through Samaria" (4:4).

*What is the goal of making a woman face her sin?

No matter how much your sin has evolved into your very identity, you can be set free. You are not bound by the image you've chosen. You don't have to continue being that person simply because that is how everyone knows you.

Remember Jesus' words: If you would ask me for what is living, I would give it to you. Jesus doesn't look at us with eyes of judgment. He knew when He came to earth that we were saturated with sin. No surprises there. He's neither shocked nor horrified. He came to set us free.

He came to set *you* free.

He looks much deeper than what others see on the surface of you. He looks at your history and understands your disappointments. He looks at your future and knows your potential. Most of all, Jesus looks at your heart, stripped from the layers that have formed around it, and He loves you with an intensity you'll never fully understand.

The Samaritan woman felt the weight of His mercy. Jesus' compassion in its true form, not the way we've contrived it, is staggering. He kindly, plainly revealed her history.

How would you *think* she'd respond to Jesus' graphic knowledge of her past?

But what does her response in John 4:19 tell you about what it is really like to encounter Jesus?

To be stripped of our sinful identities in front of Jesus doesn't bring disgrace. It simply offers Him the bare essence of our souls and allows Him to clothe us with forgiveness, godliness, and honor. It is clear that there is no condemnation between Jesus and a woman who faces her sin.

The Samaritan woman shows us what to do. She didn't run. She didn't deny. She didn't justify. She stood in front of Jesus under the weight of the truth and declared Him divinely appointed. Her confession of His holiness paved the way for Jesus to set her free. She got real with Jesus after He got real with her. That moment of truth was worth every moment of freedom that came after it.

Do you need to stand bare in front of Jesus? Will you allow Him to reveal the sin that has defined you? Accept this moment of truth, own your part, and prepare to be set free.

DAY FOUR

The Road Is Cleared

Girls, let's take a good look today at Jesus—not the way we've crafted Him but the way He really was. Because we identify so easily with the Samaritan woman, we sometimes envision the way we'd like Jesus to restore her. Certainly we love His nonjudgmental manner. We adore the way He threw off social conventions to engage her in conversation. The whole confrontation feels good. We imagine a fatherly hug, an installment of "You go, Girl!"—maybe even a round of Kum-by-yah.

But if Jesus had simply allowed her to throw off her worldly identity without giving her a new one, where would she have been? She would have been like many of us. Our question becomes: If I'm not who culture says I am, if I'm not who my gender says I should be, if I'm not who sin has shaped me to be, then who am I? Those are pretty much our defining factors, give or take a few. What's left?

After declaring Jesus a prophet, our friend went straight to a spiritual matter that had caused dissention between the Samaritans and Jews for hundreds of years. She had rightly determined that He was worthy of answering the question.

Read John 4:19-20. Do you see any of her old identity surfacing with this question? What was she still holding onto?

Here we get to see Jesus in all His glory: tender, yet so intense. He had peeled back this woman's layers one by one, and now it was time to redefine her. Having already demonstrated His acceptance of her, Jesus now spoke to her in strength. He didn't tiptoe around her fragility. He didn't water down her next step. He didn't try to ease her into real identity. He hit it hard and directly.

Read John 4:21-24. According to Jesus, what did she have wrong? How had she missed the boat?

*What insignificant aspects of worship do we get caught up in today?

Isn't this interesting? Jesus didn't say one word about atoning for her mistakes. He didn't mention anything about "healthy relationships"—a lecture she was past due on. Rather than talk about who she should become, He talked about how she should worship. Girls, there is our answer.

Jesus knew exactly how to change her broken, sinful identity. He took her gaze from inward, where she had a constant glance at shame and oppression, to outward, where she was finally able to focus on the Author of worth. It wasn't a tender message of lovey-dovey butterflies and sugar bears. Jesus said, "Believe me, woman." He explained a paradigm shift in simple terms and the message was clear: You can concentrate on Me or on you. Choose.

The longer we center on self, the deeper our identity will spiral. My pastor calls it "the paralysis of analysis." But to spend your attention on Jesus is to fill your mind with truth, value, and worship. In His presence, your identity is quickly boiled down to its core: A woman invited to worship her Savior.

He's invited those He loves.

He's invited those He values.
He's invited those who will worship.

How does your self-image affect the way you worship?

How does the way you worship affect your self-image?

A woman focused on Christ becomes full of Him. A woman who is full of Christ has a healthy identity. To know Him, to worship Him, to spend time in His presence is to slowly become like Him. That's why Jesus told the Samaritan woman His Father seeks true worshipers — those who worship in spirit and truth. Those are the ones who are free to move forward.

What do you think Jesus meant by "worship in spirit"?

What did He mean by "worship in truth"?

I think women have a unique capacity for worshiping in spirit. The problem comes in neglecting the other half: truth. True worshipers love God, fully knowing they've been invited there. They reject the lies they've been fed on their unworthiness to stand before Christ. Their worship is not tainted by selfish feelings of inadequacy or shame. They are free to focus fully on Jesus and give Him the uninhibited worship He deserves.

Does this feel too simple to you? Do you feel like I've just said, "Refocus! Forget about that other stuff," as if it doesn't need to be dealt with? No doubt deep wounds that have formed our identities must be uncovered and allowed to heal. But the way to do that is to engage in *true worship*.

That's what Jesus said anyway. Let's look at how it worked for the Samaritan woman. Jesus' last statement to her was not who He thought *she* was, but a declaration once again of who *He* was. It sealed the deal on her life change.

Read John 4:25-26. Why do you think Jesus waited until the end of their conversation to identify Himself?

So was that enough? What about being a despised Samaritan? What about being an irrelevant woman? What about her humiliating past? Well, she'd just been engaged in true worship, and her life would never be the same. Jesus was enough to eradicate a lifetime of false definition.

Read John 4:28-30,39-42. Through her example, what value do you see in a healthy identity in Christ?

This is the power of Jesus. In Him, there is no need for disgrace. There is only the need to exalt His name.

True worship.

Did she still have a road to travel? Sure. She had to begin the hard work of reorienting herself in Jesus. But I just know when the whispers began and the dark memories crept in, she said to herself: I was worthy of a conversation with Jesus. He counted me valuable. He called me to true worship, so worship I will.

You are valuable because Jesus made you so. To reject the worth He has given you is to lessen the worship He deserves. If you don't know how to accept that value, here's a hint: It begins with Jesus—not you. The longer you adore and honor Christ, the more He can graft a godly identity into your heart. If He could take the Samaritan woman from a defective faith, a lifetime of oppression, and a spirit full of sin to a bold, confident, grace-filled evangelist, changing her world in *one* conversation, just think what He can do with you.

The antidote for a flawed identity is worship. Will you worship in spirit and truth? Take some time today and focus on Christ—for who He was and who He is. Sit in His presence and be the true worshiper God seeks.

DAY FIVE

Rest Stop

Allow God's truth to infect your worship today. Learn to stand before God uninhibited by self and completely focused on Him. He knew this would be a hardship for a people so steeped in sin, so He gave us hundreds of value-builders in His Word. How gracious! He builds us up with truth to relieve us from the oppression of this world. He understands that the woman standing before Him with a healthy sense of identity is more available for true worship.

Before you dig into His Word, pray for truth today. Ask God to pierce your heart with what is real: who you really are and how He really feels about you. Pray for protection against the lies of the Enemy and embrace your identity in Christ.

Who do the following Scriptures say you are?

Isaiah 62:12

1 Corinthians 1:8

Colossians 3:12

2 Timothy 1:9

1 John 3:1

How do these Scriptures say God feels about you?

Deuteronomy 7:6

Jeremiah 31:3

Zephaniah 3:17

Luke 12:6-7

1 John 4:10

How do you respond to that? Does something inside you scream "Yes!" or "No way"? Write about what makes you believe or not believe this.

Girls, look over that list again. That is truth. God would never falsely inflate you or throw some marginal concessions your way to make you feel a little better. When He looks at you, those words reveal what He sees.

They are who you are.

Do you see how the woman who embraces this real identity is free to worship in spirit and in truth? This is cause for adoration of the Father. To accept what He has lovingly given us leaves us with no other recourse than to praise and bless His name.

If you can begin by embracing this identity, worship comes naturally. If the identity is still far off for you, begin with worship. By consistently connecting with God in praise, His Spirit is allowed the time He needs to teach you truth. To be a true worshiper is to eventually know exactly who you are in Christ.

Write out a prayer today using the phrases from the Scriptures above. Combine the truth of your identity with the worship owed to God for it ("I worship you, Father, because You counted me worthy of the loss of Your Son. Only You could make me blameless.") Write it however you see fit. If it doesn't feel true for you yet, write it anyway. Ask the Spirit to saturate you with what is real and help you cast off what is false. Pray it daily until you know it's true.

WEEK THREE

Faith

[Abram]

DAY ONE

Step One: Baby Steps

Brandon and I began ministry when we were barely old enough to spell G-O-D. While still in college, we served in a tiny church called Asher First Baptist where the head deacon was the superintendent, and the entire town shut down for every baseball game. I shudder to think about how we led those students who were basically our peers. "Clueless leading the blind" is probably too kind.

Our pastor, Adam, a former minor leaguer, stood 6 feet 4 inches or better and had this strong, authoritative presence at the pulpit. He left the baseball field for the church but still carried the same confidence he'd always known. Adam's sermons would build, and his voice would swell in crescendo.

One Sunday he was reaching the crux of his lesson, and just before he delivered the punch, he bellowed: "Now you may not believe me . . . " And before he could answer his own objection, a tiny voice from the back row, belonging to his four-year-old daughter, Autumn, spoke up in the plainest, most matter-of-fact tone: "I believe you, Daddy." She never even looked up from her coloring.

Of course we all roared, and who knows what his point was. It was so adorable, so genuine. She didn't know what he was talking about, and she couldn't have cared less that he was in the middle of his sermon. She simply wanted him to know that if no one else believed him, she did.

I believe you, Daddy.

This is what our Father wants to hear from us. This child-like confidence. This basic trust. This understanding that, even when we don't know what God is doing, we believe in Him. *We believe Him*. We don't need to know any more than that.

As we move forward, we must travel this journey of belief. Our level of trust in God informs all decisions, all relationships, all spiritual growth. Deep faith is indicative of a life deeply lived, just as surely as shallow faith points to a life lived in the wading pool of God's possibilities. I propose that a person who doesn't passionately trust God doesn't know Him very well. To really know God is to believe Him, because there is simply nothing unbelievable about Him. He *is* faithfulness. His word is covenant. His promise is absolute.

But there is a period between first meeting Him and *knowing* Him when our faith will stand or fall. There is a beginning stage of intimacy when God knows us completely, but we know only a little of Him. Maybe we meet Him as "Savior." Maybe "Restorer" or "Healer." Perhaps He is "Forgiver" or "Peace-Giver." We encounter Him on a certain level, because He meets us where we are. He is to you who you need Him to be in order to coax you to salvation.

Just as faith lies at the foundation of our spiritual journey, it also forms the beginning of God's holy Word. Barely ten pages into the Bible, we meet Abram.

Read Genesis 11:27–12:1. See if you can figure out the members of this family tree.

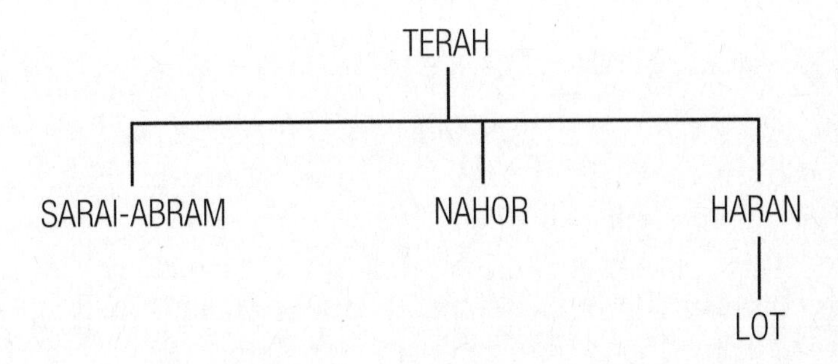

Abram grew up in Ur, capital of the mini-empire Sumer, civilized and progressive compared to the nomadic Semites that wandered the wilderness. Ur prided itself on its agricultural and architectural superiority. Priests climbed its temple-tower, or ziggurat, into the sky to offer both animal and human sacrifices to the moon god, Nanna. Sumerians were literate, educated, mathematically advanced. Their pagan culture embraced sexual perversions of all kinds. Their gods dictated all life, all death, and everything in between.[1]

This was Abram's childhood and adolescence. He grew up practicing idol worship (see Joshua 24:2). This was all he knew. We can't even assume Abram knew *of God,* which makes him unremarkable initially. He was a product of his environment, like his peers. Without God's intervention, Abram would have gone the way of his father and died an idolater.

But this was not Abram's story. This was God's story, and He had other plans.

I so wish there was a chapter between 11 and 12. Somehow the story jumps from a typical family in pagan Ur (see Genesis 11:28) to: "The LORD *had* said to Abram, 'Leave your country, your people and your father's household and go to the land I will show you'" (see Genesis 12:1).

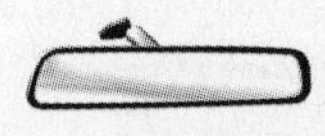

*Imagine yourself as Abram, the average guy herding sheep in pagan Ur. You get these promises and instructions from a god named "the LORD." What goes through your mind?

As far as we can tell, God did not choose Abram because of his godly virtues at this stage. In fact, this appears to be their first meeting. Here we see Abram's faith in its infancy. It is untested, unproven, uncertain. All Abram knows is that a God unlike the ones he grew up worshiping has called him. His father's gods never spoke his name, never manifested themselves so intimately, never showed themselves to be more than works of stone. This is a special calling from a special God, and it marks the beginning of his faith.

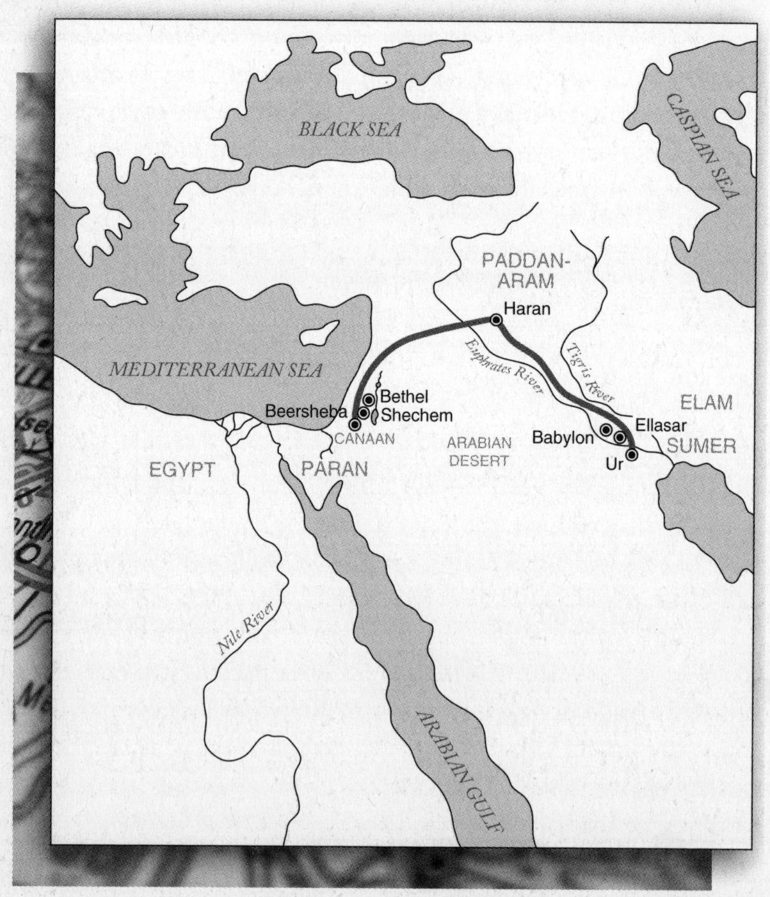

ABRAM'S JOURNEY TO CANAAN

Girls, you and I are not chosen on our merits either. Grace is purely grace and it stands alone. God still draws people to Himself based on nothing but His favor. He plucked Abram out of sinful Ur and made him the father of many nations. Abraham goes on to represent our pillar of faith in Scripture, but it didn't begin with his faith. . . it began with *God's* faithfulness.

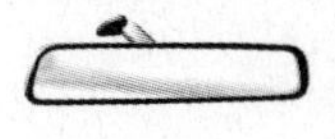
What was your life like when God first called your name?

Here is the truth: Faith doesn't originate with you; it is the obvious response to God, the center of trustworthiness. There was much work done before you and I ever had the chance to say, "I believe." God has been busy with the work of redemption since Genesis. Faith is centered in the faithfulness of *God*. Without His unwavering, undisputed faithfulness to us, there would be no discussion of our response. There would be nothing to have faith in.

What promises did God make to Abram at the beginning of his faith in Genesis 12:2-3?

Genesis 11:30 tells us that Abram's marriage was childless, and he and Sarai were both past their prime. Yet God said, "I will make you into a great nation" (12:2). What does that say to you about God?

Girls, these promises were unnecessary. One strong, swift command from God's authoritative voice should have been enough. Later, the sound of His voice caused Abraham's descendants to fear for their very lives just for hearing it (see Deuteronomy 5:25). But do you see what God was doing? He was laying a foundation of *His* faithfulness in order to launch Abram's faithfulness.

He does the exact same thing for us. He sent His Son to die in our place. That should be enough. Every human with a beating heart should launch a life of purest faith based on Jesus' sacrifice alone.

(Optional) But according to the following Scriptures, what does God promise us at the *beginning* of our faith journey?

Psalm 37:4

Psalm 91:14

Jeremiah 29:11

Look over those promises. If you believe, this is your future. When our journey of faith is young, God tells us, "Look at what I have in store for you. It is safe to move forward."

Faith becomes about us, because we discolor it with humanity. We misplace our trust and suffer the consequences. Betrayal and disappointment keep us from believing in anything or anyone wholeheartedly. We look at faith in God through this lens, and belief becomes a function of how much we're willing to risk.

*What, if anything, keeps you from believing God?

How has trusting the wrong things affected the extent of your faith in God?

If your faith has remained in its infancy, let's begin the work of growing it up. This week, let's get it properly centered on the one who is called Faithful and True (see Revelation 19:11). Hear this: Faith is not about what you do. It's about believing what God can do. Once you really believe what God can do, your life will never be the same.

Spend some time in prayer asking God to reveal the state of your faith. If your faith in God is discolored by human betrayal or misplaced trust, confess that and ask God for a clean slate. Remember where God found you, and begin the work of centering your trust in *His* faithfulness, not your version of it.

DAY TWO

Step Two: Beware of Alternate Routes

I want you to be encouraged as we continue with Abram's journey. God has made faith a journey, not an automatic destination. He pulls us along gently, giving us more and more as we can handle it. If your faith is young and untested like Abram's, watch today how God took him through a progression of growth, and be comforted that He will strengthen your faith step-by-step, too.

So He called Abram out of Ur. Wow. Let's just stop there for a second. Who in their right mind would do this? Ur, though wholly sinful, was a great place to live. It was a flourishing city, recognized in power. Had Abram confided in his fellow Sumerians what "God" told him to do, they would have declared him mad. Leave the superiority of Ur and travel 1,500 miles to Canaan? Rumors had it the Canaanites didn't even bury their dead and ate raw meat like animals![2] Nice knowing you, Abram, you nut job.

Every comfort, both material and intellectual, was available to Abram in Ur. At the bare minimum, it was home, and that was a big deal in a tribal culture where family was everything and no one simply moved away.

That brings us to the second step in this progression. Faith *begins* with God's goodness. It is launched when you say, "I believe," and supported by absolute promises. But there is reciprocal work to be done in order to grow. It is absolutely necessary.

Abram's faith journey would have halted had he stayed in Ur. God called his name, whispered his blessed future, and told him to go. Tag. You're It. Faith cannot progress outside of intentional obedience. In order to discover that God was faithful, Abram had to walk the path he was called to. God gave him what he could handle, and waited for Abram to respond.

He didn't saddle Abram with the entire vision yet. Abram was a baby faith-walker. He said, "Go. I'll show you where later. Just walk. Trust Me."

Has God called you to a specific step of faith? If so, what is it?

If you haven't taken the step, is there something you're waiting for? What is it?

Girls, God often gives you just enough information to get started. He knows what you can handle. He needs to find out if you are trustworthy. He's waiting for you to put one foot in front of the other until you've reached the maximum capacity of obedience. At that point, He'll give you more. Otherwise, your faith journey will come to a screeching halt.

We can take our cues from Abram's example. Read Genesis 12:4. I love this. So casual. So nonchalant. As if it wasn't an enormous undertaking to pack the entirety of his belongings and family, leave the comforts of the city, and start a new life as a sojourner with no home. Even in his spiritual infancy, Abram understood that this kind of God making these kinds of promises at least deserved a chance to prove Himself faithful. Way to go, Abram! You have exceptional pillar-of-faith potential. That first step was a doozy.

*What does Abram's response to God's command tell you about him?

Oh, wait one second. Did you know Abram had a little stall out on his journey? Turns out even our pillar had some faith issues. I can relate. According to Acts 7:2, God first called Abram to leave while he was still in Ur.

At that point, what three things did God tell Abram to leave behind in Genesis 12:1?

Yet Genesis 11:31 plainly tells us that Abram took two uninvited guests as he left Ur: his father, Terah, and his nephew, Lot.

The mom in me wants to let it go. Let him have his family! Let them come! Terah's old. Lot's an orphan. What's the harm? Are You just being mean? Turns out, God was just being all-knowing. He's prone to that. Why are we quick to capitalize on God's promises but slow to obey His judgment? He gave Abram the information he needed, which included journeying alone *for a reason*.

It turns out, Abram's dad and nephew created all kinds of roadblocks for him.

Read Genesis 11:31 and find the places named there on the map on page 74. Find:

- Ur, where Abram started out
- Canaan, his destination according to God's instructions
- Haran, where he stopped off for some unknown number of years

What does the map tell you about what happened to Abram's road trip with God?

*Look again at Genesis 11:31–12:5. What clues do you see in the text about why they stayed for years in Haran? How might Abram's uninvited guests have played a part?

Someone invented an alternate route, and my bets are on Terah. It sounds like Abram neglected the authority he'd been given altogether. This trip was about to get seriously uncomfortable, because Haran was the last stop of civilization before they encountered the real wilderness. And what a lucky day! Haran was a center for moon-god worship, just like Ur.[3] Felt like home.

Became a home.

Guess what happened? They fell back into their comforts, their idolatry, and Abram abandoned his faith journey for a looooong time. So long that Scripture tells us "they settled there" enough years for Terah to die and the family to accumulate a ton of possessions and people (11:31). They didn't leave Haran until Abram was seventy-five years old.

Oh yeah. Canaan.

Abram had thought: Big deal. I'll just bring my dad along. What can it hurt? Lot's only my nephew. Hey, God has two words for you, Abram: Sodom and Gomorrah. Lot's going to give you two an introduction. *God knew best.* He told Abram to journey alone. That little act of disobedience slowed his faith journey down for so long, he was an old man when he finally remembered God's calling.

*Are you on an alternate route? Has your faith journey stalled out from disobedience? Is there an area where you are favoring comfort over calling? If so, describe your situation. If not, tell why you think you're on course.

For all those years Abram lived in Haran, he could have been living in the Promised Land. He could have been enjoying his children, who would not be born while Abram was living in disobedience. He could have been experiencing God's favor.

Instead, he wasted that many years in a God-forsaken city. That many years removed from the perfection of God's plan.

Girls, the journey of faith is definitely step-by-step, but it is not a place to stop moving or invent our own route. Not only does that keep us from participating in God's holy work, but we also miss out on His best. *We miss out.* We must take what we know, what God has said to do, and walk forward in faith. Faith is demonstrated in obedience. They are exact counterparts. At some point, we have to simply move in faith, and give God the chance to show Himself faithful. He'll meet you at the next step, where He not only increases his instruction, but His favor.

God does not forsake the woman He calls. Ask God what, where, and how to move forward in faith. Ask Him to show you any weak areas. If your faith is at the same level it has been for a long time, work with the Spirit today and find out why.

DAY THREE

Step Three: Embrace the Delays

My son Gavin constantly asks to go to his favorite restaurant. McDonald's? Chick-Fil-A? Burger King? Oh no. My son loves Luby's, a cafeteria where the average patron is seventy years old and the biggest attraction is the Luann Platter. My husband and I find this hilarious, but it baffled us for years. Was our son just an old soul? Had years of McNuggets liquefied his brain, confusing him into thinking he was an eighty-year-old man who needed fiber?

We recently got to the bottom of it when I dragged him, against his will, to some fun kid's place instead of his beloved Luby's. "Honey, I don't understand. Why do you want to go to Luby's? This place has chicken shaped like dinosaurs. Someday they will embalm your innards completely, and you can park your wheelchair at Luby's and try to make up for years of eating these cancer nuggets." His answer was simple: "At Luby's, you get your food right away. No waiting."

And there it was: a basic case of instant gratification. He was oblivious to the Luby's demographic. His devotion to this geriatric cafeteria was based solely on the speed at which he could go from ordering to ingestion.

We're not a patient people. It begins at infancy and continues to spiral down until the car in front of us waits approximately .02 seconds to move after the light has turned green and we honk our horn and yell mean things like, "Pay attention! This is not a parking lot!" and our kids ask us if there is another idiot in front of us. (Oops.) We want things the way we want them, and we want them yesterday.

This often poses some difficulties on the spiritual road to faith. Clearly I'm not speaking from experience, but maybe you can relate (roll eyes here). Waiting is hard. It's unnatural. It makes us cranky and forgetful. We view it as a roadblock, not an integral part of the faith journey.

But it is.

God teaches this well through Abram. He eventually made it to Canaan after his self-imposed detour. I often think about him pulling into Canaan with his enormous posse, none too happy with that journey, I'm sure. Well, here we are! I guess we should . . . uh . . . check it out, or uh . . . pitch a tent or something. This is it, right? I told you He said 'Canaan,' right? *God?*

The ball had been in Abram's court for quite a while, and now it was God's turn. God hadn't told him anything other than "go to a place I will show you," and now he was there with no other instructions. A kind of scary place to be. That place where you want some reassurance that you *weren't* crazy and you *did* hear God. After all, it had been a long time since God first called him.

Right away, what did God promise again in Genesis 12:7, face-to-face, no less?

What do you think went through Abram's mind at this point?

Perhaps Abram thought he had arrived. Maybe he thought the end of the journey was the end of this deal. I bet he started looking around for all those promises. But God had some growing up planned for Abram's young faith.

Briefly summarize what Abram did in each of the following episodes. Include *why* he did it, if you can tell from the text.

Genesis 12:10-20

Genesis 13:1-18

Genesis 14:8-20

Alrighty then. So the "Promised Land" was occupied and apparently void of food, Pharaoh wanted to kill him so he could sleep with Sarai (so Abram passed her off as his sister. . . still working on that pillar status), he got kicked out of Egypt back to Famineland, the herdsmen were fighting, Lot picked the best land in Canaan, then had to be rescued when it turned into a war zone. Meanwhile, no sign of a baby. Lovin' it here, God. Thanks. This is much better than Ur.

This is the walk of faith. The zeal of beginning the journey has faded. The fulfillment of the vision is still far off. Will you still believe when it gets hard? Will you still believe when there are delays? Will you still believe when the promise is unseen? I'm quick to hate this stage. I want to be annoyed and confused by it. I want to jump ship right about this time. I may even get mad at God and try to boss Him just a little bit.

Summarize what Abram was feeling in Genesis 15:1-3.

*Can you relate? If so, how?

We want to write this all off as God being difficult, or at best, a dry season to endure, a miserable time to suffer through. But let's go back. All along the way, God was using every last trial, each postponement, to build Abram's faith and to reveal Himself more and more. God knew Abram's greatest test was yet to come, and he wasn't ready for it.

Scripture shows us how God carried him through each obstacle. Abram emerged from these "delays" much stronger, much richer, more esteemed, secure, and favored. God didn't allow one circumstance to fall to the ground. Each one was used to advance this faith journey.

*What do you think Abram learned about God from these delays?

The Abram we see here is not the same one who began this journey. The relationship between him and God had progressed to new heights. God had taken him through many stages of the journey, allowing Abram to practice trusting while God displayed His faithfulness. A beautiful cycle had emerged.

Are you in the middle of the faith journey somewhere, feeling stuck? If so, what do you think God is doing?

*How are you dealing with God in the middle of this situation?

How is He dealing with you?

Girls, God waits to sustain you on your faith journey. We can't question His timing or the delivery of His promises. Rest assured, His timing is better than yours. Sometimes the journey forward is held up by our own sinful detours, but if you've done a thorough check of your spirit and you stand clean, the "delay" might be God's doing for the purpose of growing your faith up. He alone knows what lies ahead of you, and He alone knows how to prepare you.

Submit to this leg of the faith trip. Rather than pine away for the destination, choose to learn from every step along the way, even the ones that are uphill. It just might be that God is waiting for you to embrace each segment in faith so He can bring you into your own Canaan. Will you choose to believe what you can't yet see? Are you willing to make a *sacrifice of faith* against your comforts, against your time frame? Declare this to be not a season to endure, but a season to advance your faith, and God will carry you "from strength to strength" (Psalm 84:7) until your trust is mature and complete.

Pray earnestly to God, expressing where you are right now and what you need from Him.

DAY FOUR

Step Four: The Bridge of Sacrifice

We are going to fast forward in Abram's story. We're skipping some very special parts, but skim with me. God gave Abram a son, Ishmael, through Sarai's maidservant. They really messed this up terribly, yet God still loved them and promised to bless Ishmael's descendants as Abram requested. For Abram's sake alone, God spared his nephew Lot from the destruction of Sodom and Gomorrah. (Lot was such a pain. Really should have left him in Ur.) He changed their names to Abraham and Sarah, symbolically preparing them for the ultimate promise that began with the blessed birth of Isaac at the ripe old age of one hundred. Yeah, God!

How would you describe the relationship between Abraham and God that you've seen so far?

We need to get our arms around the longevity of their relationship to endure what comes next. I know you want to skip it. I once did, too. The narrator of Genesis is gracious in his choice of words. He tells us: "Some time later God *tested* Abraham"

(22:1). As if he knew we might simply pass out at the command if we didn't know it was only a test.

Read God's words to Abraham in Genesis 22:2. What do you feel when you read this?

The first time I read this story myself, not the G-rated church version, I threw my Bible on the ground and cried for an hour. No, God! No! Not Isaac! They'd waited so long! They loved him so much! Why are you so mean, God? This is the meanest thing I've ever read! *Ever*. How are we to make sense of this? How can we endure this story? How can this be the God we love?

For generations, this story has been labeled "The Story of *Abraham's* Faith in God." Will he obey? Will he do the unthinkable? Will he prove himself faithful regardless of the task? I agree on the title, but I'd make a slight emphasis change. This is "The Story of Abraham's Faith *in God*."

Much is made of Abraham throughout this part of the story. We assume his feelings, his fear, his horror, his devastation, though the Bible records none of that. This is how we view Abraham because this is how *we* feel. We transfer this moment to our own lives, our faith, but it can never make the leap. I've yet to meet a woman who's shaken her fist at our revulsion and said, "I could have done it."

But this is not our story. This was between God and Abraham. We are simply given a glimpse inside their journey. I truly believe from the bottom of my heart that in this moment, in this horrific command, God was not the only one who knew Isaac would be spared. I believe Abraham knew, too.

What exactly did God say earlier to Abraham in Genesis 17:19?

Given their history, how do you think Abraham viewed this promise?

God wasn't being mean asking for Isaac. He *knew* Abraham believed Him fully. He *knew* Abraham trusted he'd see Isaac grow up. He *knew* Abraham wouldn't be terrified. It was almost like a private discussion between the two of them. A hidden agenda only they understood.

"Sacrifice Isaac."

"I know you wouldn't have me do that."

"I know you know. Will you take steps to obey me anyway?"

"You know I will."

"Of course I know you will."

This isn't my own interpretation to offer relief from this story.

Read Genesis 22:1-19. How did Abraham demonstrate his secure belief while taking steps to obey in the following verses?

Genesis 22:5

Genesis 22:7-8

Abraham's belief was confirmed in two major omissions. When God's command first came:

1. Abraham asked no questions, required no clarity. This was not the way of his past. He'd questioned God about:

- His promise of a son (see Genesis 15:1-3)
- His promise of Canaan (see Genesis 15:8)
- His provision through Isaac rather than Ishmael (see Genesis 17:17-20)
- His destructive plans for Sodom (see Genesis 18:22-33)

2. He didn't tell Sarah. He just left with Isaac.

*What does Abraham's silence in this passage communicate to you?

There lies a gap between "knowing about God's faithfulness" and "knowing God's faithfulness." The bridge is constructed by sacrifice. Your journey of faith requires a different sacrifice than mine. For me, I've had to sacrifice fear in order to know God's faithfulness. I can obtain it absolutely no other way. There comes a point of, well, faith. Believing what we can't see or understand or plan for or be tangibly assured of this side of the sacrifice.

*What must you sacrifice to trust God? Your desires? Control? Confident façade? Comforts? Why is this sacrifice hard for you to make?

Here's what's so endearing about God. He often gives us back tenfold what we're willing to sacrifice. Sacrifice your pride; become exalted by God Himself. Sacrifice your fear; become secure in the hands of the Almighty Creator. Sacrifice your pain; be healed by the loving touch of Jesus. Not only do we emerge stronger and better, but we find ourselves advancing down the road of maturity. Each sacrifice brings a better promise. Each better promise strengthens our faith. A strengthened faith allows the next sacrifice to be easier. And so it goes.

James later explained Abraham's faith to us: "His faith and his actions were working together, and his faith was made complete by what he did. . . .and he was called God's friend" (James 2:22-23).

If this is true, what does your current level of faith communicate about your level of obedience?

Abraham was willing to obey, and God not only spared Isaac but established the twelve tribes of Israel through Isaac's son, Jacob. Remember, God didn't give this test in Abram's first precarious years. He didn't ask for this while Abram was still taking detours and passing his wife off as his sister. He waited until Abraham's faith was mature. Abraham had made many sacrifices along his road to faith, and they had all been returned to him. This was one more (albeit a doozy) on the path to maturity, and Abraham trusted the outcome. Because he trusted the God who was in control of the outcome. And his "faith was made complete."

How do you feel about putting God in charge of your outcomes? Can you pinpoint why you feel that way?

We look on in horror because our faith has not been established like Abraham's. We identify with his earlier years, the disobedient and whiny ones. This grown-up faith, this unquestioning trust, feels foreign. So we can't understand what happens between God and a man who believes Him infinitely. But this isn't a picture of cruelty. It's a demonstration of the ultimate bond between God and mankind when we are willing to believe Him above all else.

Believers, it was on this same mountain that later became Jerusalem where Solomon's temple was built. It was in this same city where God, not withholding *His* one and only Son, the one *He* loved, offered Jesus as the sacrificial lamb for me. For you. Our place was on that altar. Where He spared Isaac, He sacrificed Jesus. He has never put a yoke on mankind He wasn't willing to endure. Abraham was given back Isaac, his laughter (see Genesis 17:17), where Jesus cried out and gave up His spirit.

Don't be angry at God for this story. This has been a place of God's mercy, presence, and faithfulness from Abraham to Solomon to Jesus. The theme of this mountain is faithful sacrifice: Abraham was willing and was spared, Jesus was willing and was offered—by the same God whose laughter is His people and who loves to call us "friends."

Girls, our faithful sacrifices pale in comparison to God's. Will you move forward? Will you believe Him? He is worthy of your belief. Thank God for this story. Ask Him to teach you the truth of believing in Him.

DAY FIVE

Rest Stop

Girls, faith is entirely valuable to God. He esteems it higher than almost any other quality we exhibit. He searches for the woman who says, "I believe You, Daddy," and rains down the impossible on her life. He can use her, trust her, lead her, confide in her, stretch her. She is moldable clay in His perfect hands.

Will you be her? Will you believe God? Will you believe He knows better than you do? Will you obey and sacrifice to know God's faithfulness? Will you take that risk? Walk with me through a beautiful psalm of faith, and let's offer it to the God of faithfulness.

Turn to Psalm 20. As you work through it in sections, spend a few minutes in prayer before responding to each part. Be honest with God, and ask Him to shine His light of truth on your heart. After praying, respond to Scripture through journaling. For each section, write a paragraph of prayer to God or reflection about your life. Some questions you might ask yourself are included below, but you should treat them as springboards to your own thoughts.

Read Psalm 20:1-2.

- Is your faith in distress? Is it young, not yet moved? Is it stuck in a detour of your choosing? Is it suffering through waiting? Is it being fiercely tested?
- Have you asked for help? Have you sought support from the Spirit? From your travel companions? Is your sustainer the God of Abraham's grandson, Jacob? What do you need to do to secure help on this road to faith?

Read Psalm 20:3.

- What do you need to sacrifice in order to demonstrate your belief? An attitude? A sin? A hurt? Complacency? Ask God to accept your sacrifice and advance your faith.

Read Psalm 20:4-5.

- Do you believe that God wants to give you joy? Do you believe that His plans are to prosper you and not to harm you? Have you mistaken sacrificial faith as oppressive? Do you hold back because you fear you will lose yourself? Your dreams? How do these verses portray God in this light? How will you respond?

Read Psalm 20:6.

- Do you *know* God saves his chosen? Have you heard His faithful answers? Have you rested in the safety of His right hand? Remember what God has done for you. Where has He brought you from? How has He been faithful? Give Him the specific credit He deserves. Allow His history to fuel your future faith travel.

Read Psalm 20:7-8.

- What "chariot" or "horse" have you trusted in? How did it bring you to your knees? How did it make you fall? Will you decide to trust in God's name? Will you cement it in actions? Will you choose to believe that, through your faith, He will raise you up until you stand firm like Abraham?

I pray this week you were able to journey forward on the faith road. This requires much travel, but it begins one mile at a time. Take the next step this very day. Move forward. Grow in faith, Girls. It's safe to risk it. God hasn't failed once.

> *I know whom I have believed,* and am convinced that he is able to guard what I have entrusted to him for that day. (2 Timothy 1:12)

WEEK FOUR

Discipleship

[PETER]

DAY ONE

Leaving the Nets

Kelly had big, curly blonde hair. She wore the coolest clothes and the best Jordache jeans. She was engaged to Davy Crockett—a descendant of the *real one*. I hung on her every word. No one her age talked to me like a friend. She was my favorite babysitter, and I wanted to be exactly like her. I was eight.

I tried to make my lame clothes somehow look like hers. I prayed every night that my stringy, dishwater hair would turn platinum and curly by dawn. I studied the way she walked and practiced in my bedroom. I achieved less "Kelly Pace" and more "baby giraffe with two hip replacements on cocaine." She was my idol.

It is in our nature to admire others. As young women, we often seek out mentors to shape us and model good living for us. Our eyes constantly seek those we'd like to pattern ourselves after. That's who I want to be like. She's a great example for me. In our journey of faith, a mentor with skin and bones gives us a tangible model to learn from.

This is a great concept. Brilliant, actually. Jesus thought so, too. In fact, the entire gospel rested on the assumption that His young protégés would study His life and ultimately imitate what they saw. Do what I do. Love how I love. Teach like I teach. Demonstrate My courage. Learn from My strength. Carry on My message.

We have lots of terms for this: spiritual growth / development / maturity / equipping. Give the modern church a couple of more years and we'll come up with another. But my favorite word is the same one Jesus used: discipleship. Girls, if we all decided to take this particular journey, we would change the entire world. To become more like Jesus is our highest goal, the ultimate tribute to His extraordinary life.

Jesus put it plainly in John 8:12: "I am the light of the world. Whoever *follows me* will never walk in darkness, but will have the light of life."

As we explore the journey of discipleship, we're going to walk alongside one of the chosen Twelve. Some of the most fortunate and blessed of all believers, these men were the ones who knew Jesus with skin and bones. The ones who knew the sound of His voice and the strong grip of His hands. The ones He called by name and mentored around the clock and loved as brothers. We're going to travel forward with my favorite disciple, Peter. Let's learn from him as he learned from Jesus.

First, a quick history lesson (I promise you'll think this is cool in just a minute): In Galilee, where Jesus and Peter both grew up, religious education began in the synagogue at about age five. These children were taught by a local rabbi and learning primarily focused on the Torah, the first five books of the Bible. Their job was to read, write, and memorize Scripture. That was school. "Separation of church and state" would've given the Jews a coronary. This education lasted until about age thirteen. At that point, most boys left the synagogue to learn the family trade.

Only the very best students continued under the rabbi to study the remainder of the Hebrew Bible. At about eighteen, most of those completed this formal education and developed their trade. But the teeniest percentage of them—the brightest, most capable young men—entered the highest level of education: becoming a rabbi's disciple.

This small handful of young men sought permission to study with a famous rabbi, and they would leave their homes to live and travel with him full-time. In those days, to become a rabbi was the highest possible honor. So to be chosen to study with one was a very close second. It was a spiritual privilege unmatched in the first century and only bestowed on the most brilliant boys with the greatest potential for imitation.

They would come to know their rabbi like a father. They followed him every minute of every day, closely observing his every word and action. Their ultimate goal was to one day be a carbon copy of their rabbi—duplicating his methods and carrying forth his brand of teaching. The rabbi-disciple relationship was wholly intimate, reciprocating complete faith in each other.[1]

You can be sure our Peter wasn't in this elite group. He studied, no doubt, and knew a lot of Scripture as all young Jewish men did, but he was a fisherman. At some point, his education ended and he accepted his lot in life on the sea.

Read John 1:35-41. What are some basic facts or characteristics you can glean about Peter and Andrew from this passage?

Following John the Baptist was a good sign. He was Jesus' cousin sent straight from God to prepare for Jesus' ministry. If anyone was on the right track, it was John the B. He spoke of God's Son, the Savior of the world. He was utterly humble and faithfully directed his disciples' attention to the coming Jesus. Good man.

Read John 1:42. Peter studied the Torah, where God changed Abram's name to Abraham, Sarai to Sarah, Jacob to Israel—pillars of his faith. So what might have gone through Peter's mind when Jesus said this?

Boring holes into Peter's eyes, Jesus already knew him: You *are* Simon son of John. I know you. And in the same breath, he spoke to Peter's future: You *will be* called Cephas. I know who you'll become. He gave Peter the Aramaic name for "rock," though he had done nothing yet to warrant a name change. This is the Jesus I know. The moment He engages us, we are known completely. Past, present, and future.

*How does it make you feel to be known completely by Jesus?

Being known is one thing, but it doesn't automatically translate to discipleship, because we are all known completely, yet only a few risk being followers. Peter had a slow start, too. He met Jesus and even got a new name, a new destiny. Yet it wasn't until later that he became a disciple.

Peter went back to his boat for a short season, and Jesus had to engage him a second time. Read Luke 5:1-11. Why do you think Peter said what he did in verse 8?

Perhaps his delayed response was due to the shocking nature of this unconventional calling. There he was: a simple fisherman, educated at only basic levels, now rocketed forward to the elite group of "disciples." And not just of any rabbi. He was invited by the Messiah to leave all behind, follow Him, learn from Him, know Him closer than family. This was an unbelievable turn of events. Jesus believed in Peter's potential enough to make him a disciple. Peter finally understood.

*Do you understand that Jesus has invited you to be His disciple? Do you realize He considers you worthy of the rabbi-student relationship? Where are you on the following continuum?

- I've never encountered Jesus _____
- I'm known by Him, but I'm back in my old boat _____
- Jesus is pursuing me again _____
- "Go away from me, Lord; I'm a sinful girl!" _____
- My nets are on the shore—I'm a disciple of my rabbi _____

Jesus considers you worthy because He knows *He* can instruct, empower, and fill you with His Spirit so you'll be more like Him. You are capable of imitating this rabbi with His help. You are. If He didn't believe in His followers, God would have created a different way to reach this lost world. He calls us to discipleship, because through His power, He knows we are able.

This confident journey of discipleship begins here: leaving behind our nets. Those nets represented the same things to Peter as they do to us.

What was the significance of Peter leaving behind his boat and nets to follow Jesus?

*What are your "nets"?

I'll tell you what my nets are: comforts, the approval of man, selfishness, fear of rejection, control. Those have kept me tied up for years, but they cannot come along as I follow my rabbi. Until they are all left behind, I'm not a real disciple. I'm simply meeting up with Him from time to time.

What holds you back from leaving your nets behind?

Jesus said: Follow Me. Above advancing our agendas, fulfilling our dreams, and carving out our own niche, we must follow Jesus. To know Him like family. To learn from His ministry. To share His burdens. To imitate His love.

Perhaps the best advice on how to do this comes from the Mishnah (the Jewish compilation of laws and sayings from Jesus' time). It urges: "Cover yourself in the dust of your rabbi's feet."[2]

May we all follow behind Him that closely.

Will you accept the invitation to be a disciple of Jesus? Thank Jesus for finding you worthy of the calling. Spend some time praying about what to leave behind, and ask for courage to begin the journey behind Jesus.

DAY TWO

Follow the Rabbi

Ah, driving school. Do you remember yours? I was a sophomore in high school, and my best friend, Nicki, and I crossed the campus to the shop building where the magic happened: Driver's Ed. Every bizarre brand of teen was in there, begging to be put in charge of a two-ton vehicle so they could inflict road trauma as soon as possible.

Our favorite Driver's Ed activity was the simulator. We'd watch a driving film blown up to lifelike proportions on the wall and maneuver a fake car. Our teacher would sit in the control booth and light up our "screw-up dashboard" as we navigated like two wasted drivers on cell phones. Somehow, we eventually made it to the "Driver's Education Car," complete with an additional brake on the passenger's floor board that my husband has made longing references to many, many times.

Alas, I did actually learn some things. I learned that "yield" means that *I* have to yield. Who knew? I learned that a blinking red light is not an optional stop after all. I learned that "two car lengths" is actually much farther than I estimated. I learned that most signs have purposes that are best fulfilled when I don't ignore them. Driving educated and informed actually has some merit. Go figure.

On the journey of discipleship, the first step is to accept the invitation and leave our nets. The second step is to get schooled by Jesus. Our faith must become informed or it runs the risk of becoming (1) reckless, (2) misguided, or (3) obsolete.

Have you been reckless, misguided, or obsolete in your faith? If so, how has your uninformed faith derailed your spiritual journey? If not, how would you describe the quality of your discipleship?

No doubt Peter was zealous to learn, as he was a fisherman with a lot of rough edges. He had a steep learning curve, but Jesus knew He didn't have much time with His disciples—only about three years to equip these guys, train them, and commit the gospel to them. Not to mention that none were scholars; none had been selected by any other rabbis as exceptional.

*Can you identify with the disciples as average? I sure can. What insecurities affect you as a chosen follower of Jesus? (Or if you don't suffer from insecurities, where does your confidence come from?)

For the sake of time, Jesus dropped his young disciples right into the deep end. Take a look at the first three things Peter saw Him do. Read Luke 5:12-32. So far, how would you describe Jesus as Peter saw Him?

So this is Jesus. Can you picture the disciples looking at each other in disbelief? Man! The other rabbis never do stuff like this! The crowds are pressing in, and the disciples are starting to figure out they've bitten off a big chunk here.

In those early moments, what lessons do you think Jesus was teaching them?

The disciples learned these lessons firsthand *by observation*. This is the rabbi-disciple model. They watched His facial expressions and witnessed His miracles. They saw the faces of those He touched. Lucky disciples. They were truly covered in the dust of their rabbi's feet.

So where does this leave us? If we're called to follow Jesus like this, what are *we* supposed to do? If I could just reach out and touch Him whenever I wanted to, I'd be a good little follower, too. I'm just sure of it. But time and distance render this model of discipleship impossible for me, right?

Wrong. I've never touched Jesus. I haven't walked down roads with Him or sat by the lake next to Him. But I know Him as closely as I know anyone with skin on. My heart aches with love for Jesus, and He leads and teaches me through the pages of my Bible.

John put it best: "The Word became flesh and made his dwelling among us" (John 1:14).

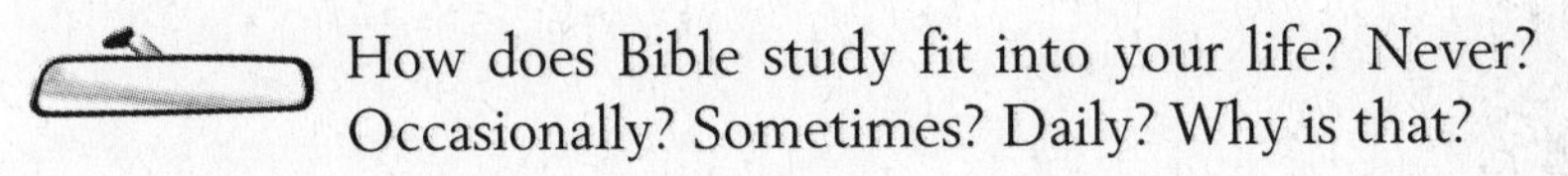

*How convinced are you that you can know Jesus intimately by regularly reading about Him in the Bible? What makes you say that?

Is your level of commitment as a disciple at about the same level as the amount of time you spend in Scripture? Or are these two things not currently related for you? Describe your experience.

The disciples set their world ablaze because they spent almost three solid years watching Jesus' every move. You cannot be unchanged by that type of commitment. By the same turn, it is almost impossible to envelop ourselves with Scripture and not become a true disciple. (Okay, it's possible to be a Bible nerd who is all about information and not about transformation. But that's not your problem, is it?) Look around. Every single believer you admire for her faith has her head buried in the Word. I guarantee it.

Glance back over Luke 5:12-32. What would your life be like if you knew in your gut that every word of this was real?

Here is a basic framework I recommend to get started:

- Pick one book to study at a time (Starters: Luke, Ephesians, 1 John)
- Ask the Holy Spirit to teach you *before* you begin studying. Invite Him to meet you.
- Set aside 30 minutes at the same time each day. If you don't schedule it, it won't happen.
- Read just a handful of verses each day. You won't learn what you can't retain.
- Don't be scared to use a helper to clear up context and history for you.
  - James S. Bell Jr. and Stan Campbell, *The Complete Idiot's Guide to the Bible*
  - Nick Page, *The MAP: Making the Bible Meaningful, Accessible, Practical*
  - John MacArthur, *The MacArthur Bible Handbook: The Ultimate Book-by-Book Survey of the Bible*
  - www.bible-history.com
- Use a journal. Write questions. Extend your thoughts. Search the application. Make a personal connection. Write out your prayers. The Bible is a conversation, not a lecture.
- Invite a partner or small group to dive in with you and meet weekly. This will keep you on track better than the threat of a bikini wax with no Advil.

Don't let fears hold you back. Remember, God values a steady pace over a sprint. Just begin. The Word may begin as black-and-white print on paper sandwiched between leather, but spend enough time there, and Jesus will become flesh. You will love and follow Him as if you could actually feel the calluses on His hands.

Offer your Bible study hang-ups to God today. Write them out. Ask the Spirit to move forward with you in discipleship. Commit to daily time in the Word. Name the time, place, book, and friend that will mark the next leg of your journey.

DAY THREE

A New Rock

What a journey discipleship is. There is never a point of "arrival." There is always more to learn, more to discover, more Jesus to love. But there are some basic stages of discipleship that all believers can progress through. We've discussed two through the example of Peter:

1. Accept the invitation to follow Jesus with abandon, leaving your nets.
2. Immerse yourself in the example of Jesus—flesh and blood for Peter, the Word for us.

It is again through Peter that we see Jesus stretch him—and us—to a new level of discipleship. The following shows what an extraordinary teacher Jesus was. After spending many months with his young disciples, Jesus knew they were ready for the next stage. He had less than one year left on earth.

From Bethsaida, He took His disciples north almost twenty-five miles to Caesarea-Philippi (see map on page 111), as we are about to read in Matthew 16. Now, let me tell you a bit about CP. First of all, it was *not* a Jewish city. It was, in fact, quite pagan. It was originally settled by a general of Alexander the

Great after his death (323 BC), and a decidedly Greek culture was established.

Back then, a cave was discovered where the snowmelt from nearby Mount Hermon flowed underground and surfaced at the base of a high rock cliff. This cave, housing one of the biggest natural springs in the Middle East, was declared sacred and dedicated to Pan, the Greek god of herds, shepherds, and nature. A cult center called Paneas ("sanctuary of Pan") was built on this site.

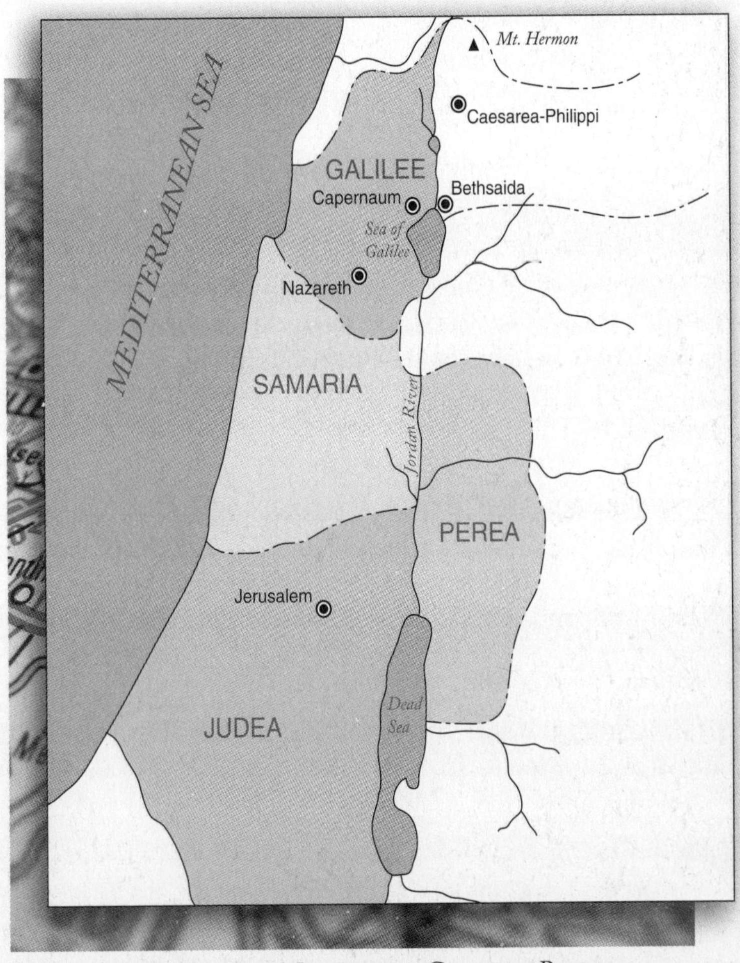

THE DISCIPLES' JOURNEY TO CAESAREA-PHILIPPI

In 20 BC, Paneas was added to the kingdom of Herod the Great, the *extremely* pro-Roman king of Judea. A year later, he built a marble temple dedicated to Augustus Caesar next to Pan's temple. In 4 BC, Herod died and Paneas became part of his son, Philip's, territory. Philip named the city "Caesarea-Philippi" and declared it the capital of his kingdom.[3] So, to sum up:

- CP had *pro-Greek* idol worship centered on a natural spring at the base of a rock cliff.
- CP had a *pro-Roman* leader who dedicated a huge shrine to Augustus.
- You'd be hard pressed to find anything *pro-Jewish*.

This was not a godly place. There was no synagogue here. This was an unlikely destination for a wandering Jewish rabbi and his disciples. We can be nearly certain they'd never set foot in godless Caesarea-Philippi. Yet, Jesus began walking north without a word. The disciples must have known where they were headed, and I bet they were freaking.

Has Jesus ever led you somewhere shocking? If so, where?

I can imagine the disciples staring at those huge pagan shrines built into the side of the rock cliff that towered over the city. They saw cult niches carved into the face of that same rock containing all kinds of idols. These people! This place! *What are we doing here?*

Jesus had an important lesson to teach them, He needed the right backdrop, and this was it. We know He didn't care about conventional protocol. So, as they stared up at that huge rock face holding all those idols and temples, Jesus finally spoke up.

Read Matthew 16:13-16. If Jesus already knew the answers, why do you think He asked these questions of His disciples?

We still have the same murmurings today. Maybe Jesus was just a great teacher, or some kind of prophet. Perhaps He was simply a social revolutionary who shook up the first century a bit. Maybe He was "a way" but not "the way." Possibly He was the Christian version of Buddha. The question Jesus asked His disciples is still being asked.

Who do *you* say Jesus is? List all the things He is to you.

Peter nailed it. You are Christ: chosen, holy, the Messiah we've been waiting for. You are the Son of the Living God: divine, supernatural, the Father's joy. Against this pagan backdrop representing all the false ways, Peter singled Jesus out as the Only Way.

*Read Matthew 16:17-19. Given the physical landscape of Caesarea-Philippi, what significance do you see in Jesus' words in verse 18?

The next level.

In fact, this is the first time Jesus used the word "church." It was such a significant development that He took them all the way to Caesarea-Philippi to intensify the message.

Jesus was authoring a radical departure from the normal. He was transitioning from the religion of the temple to the freedom gospel of His church. His precious church, carried on the backs of humble believers, not dripping from the robes of the high priests. In fact, He handed the keys not to a scholar, but to a fisherman.

Girls, you and I are the recipients of Jesus' church. He committed its welfare to all His disciples, called by name and equipped to serve. On the journey of discipleship, we are to be all about the business of Jesus' church. Just like the original disciples, we have to move from the comforts of being consumers to being servants. This is centered in the local church just as it was in the first century.

What's your relationship with a local church?

- Unassociated with any church
- Lily and poinsettia club (Easter and Christmas attendance)
- Patron of many, member of none
- Loose affiliation with one church
- Regular of a church
- Member of a church
- Serving within my church
- Practically living at my church (maybe a tad excessive)

If you're not committed to a local church, what has kept you from doing so?

As disciples, our progression should take us all the way to service (which we'll discuss at length later). Believe me, I know it's tempting to sit in the pews indefinitely and let everyone else do the church's work, but that approach has two fatal flaws: (1) The church misses out on your gifts, your talents. Someone is not being loved, cared for, or ministered to because of your absence. (2) You are missing out on the indescribable blessings of doing God's work. There is a void that can only be filled by serving in the capacity you were created for.

Jesus modeled these principles at sunset just *hours* before His crucifixion. He demonstrated the final lesson to His disciples in another brilliant teaching moment. As they gathered to share in the Lord's Supper—symbolically taking ownership in Jesus' ministry—He taught them specifically how to fulfill their new calling.

Read John 13:1-17. What misconceptions about service might have fueled Peter's responses in verses 6 and 8?

*What misconceptions do you have about serving in the church?

*What does it mean to wash each other's feet today?

Jesus made it clear in verse 15: "I have set you an example that you should do as I have done for you." Wash each other's feet. Serve the other believers in your life. This is how to have a part in Jesus' legacy. This is what disciples do through His church. We work in the nursery. We greet at the front door. We facilitate a small group. We take meals to those who need them. We go as a sponsor to youth camp. We minister to the broken in our community. We serve in the way we know best.

Listen, a healthy church is a huge machine, and it takes a ton of oil to keep moving forward. That oil doesn't come from a wave of Jesus' magic wand. It comes from the obedience of His disciples. Because we want to be like Him. Because He set that example for us. Because in it we get to take part in His ministry. Because we are His followers.

What is your next step in this journey? Regular attendance? Membership? Becoming a volunteer? What will you do?

Jesus established His church as a local group of believers who would learn together, grow up together, and serve each other and their community. It is a beautiful plan. "No servant is greater than his master." If Jesus' last hours were worthy of service, could our time be spent any better? Jesus' church is nothing less than the hope of the world.

Join the party.

Prayerfully consider your next move. Ask God for wisdom and courage to move forward in discipleship. Thank Jesus for allowing you to take part in His ministry. What a privilege.

DAY FOUR

A Commissioning

My dad, bless his heart. There he was, a man's man, an outdoorsman really. He'd grown up with one brother, no sisters. He was into cars, sports, hanging with his boys. He ruined every one of Mom's wedding pictures by sporting a vicious sunburn from playing a ball tournament up until one hour before his blessed nuptials, which, frankly, were number two on his list that day. And what did he get? Three daughters in a row. We might have been girlish, but who knows? Dad put softball gloves in our fat little baby hands and hoped for the best. Even lying wounded on the softball field as little girls, we'd hear Dad yell from the stands, "Don't rub it!" We were boys with ponytails.

But you have to hand it to him—it worked. He managed to wrangle athleticism out of three dramatic daughters. We grew up on the ball field just as he did. And if you'll indulge me a small confession, I now whisper to my sparkle-filled, glittery, dreamer daughter: "Baby, you're going to be the best softball player."

There are certain things we simply want to pass on. We want others to know the joys we've known. We want someone else to share in our favorite experiences. We want to point others down the good paths we've walked. Sometimes we feel so compelled to do this that it becomes our mission.

In the rabbi-disciple relationship, the ultimate goal for each trained disciple was to seek out new followers who would adopt his message and imitate him, just as he imitated his rabbi. This was the principle of multiplication: The message would reproduce and spread until it reached the world. As disciples, this is the ultimate fulfillment of our responsibilities.

*How do you honestly feel about sharing your faith?

If you said anything negative at all, I hear you, Sister. We've made a mess of this level of discipleship, in my opinion. We've made it stiff and awkward and canned. Even worse, we've made it forced. So let's back up and talk about what it should look like.

In the early stages, Jesus centered His ministry in Capernaum, a city in Galilee that He called home (see Mark 2:1). He spent a lot of time teaching in the synagogue there, but three separate times He traveled the countryside of Galilee teaching to crowds. On the third tour, the disciples were sent out on their own to practice ministering as they'd seen Jesus do.

Read Luke 9:1-6. What concerns do you think the disciples might have had about this mission?

Do you see any similarities with your earlier answer about sharing your faith? If so, what? If not, what contrasts do you notice?

With about six months left on earth, Jesus expanded His mission again. Although the Twelve comprised His inner circle, Jesus had acquired thousands of disciples. He had blanketed Galilee with His message, and it was time to turn His gaze south toward Judea, home of Jerusalem, the pre-appointed place of his death (see map on page 111).

Read Luke 10:1-4. What do you pick up in Jesus' tone?

How do you react to the idea of being a lamb among wolves (see verse 3)?

What happens if the lambs opt to hide from the wolves?

Check out the reaction of those seventy-two upon rejoining Jesus in Luke 10:17. List three words to describe their response.

*Have you ever shared Christ with someone who accepted His grace? If so, how did it change you?

It is amazing to discover that we can indeed be like Jesus. Not in His divinity or His perfection, but in His mission. To find out that He *will* empower us through the knowledge of Him is cause for celebration. We can do what He asked us to do. What do you know? Jesus knew what He was talking about.

Perhaps even better is our Savior's reaction upon the success of our mission. Read Luke 10:21. List two or three reasons why our obedience in evangelism might bring Jesus joy.

Fellow disciples, if all we ever do is remain in the "learning stage," who will shoulder Jesus' mission? Who will take His message to the lost and broken? Oh, some of them may seem happy living in sin and authoring their own agendas, but I assure you they are not.

This is our sad world, Girls. It is full of people looking around desperately, wondering if this is all there is. It doesn't matter if their exterior looks desperate or not. Their insides are empty. And Jesus loves them so much. He died so they could know peace. He is relying on us to love them just as He would if He were still walking this earth.

Our role is mission critical, yet we prefer to let it slide. It makes us feel uncomfortable. Perhaps the root of our reluctance is how the mission strategy has been distorted. We've boxed it in and emptied it of context. We've relegated it to a tract mentality complete with a canned speech. Who wants to do that? Who wants to *hear* that?

This is no good. No wonder people think believers are weird. The rabbi-disciple model was born out of relationships. Jesus began His kingdom by walking and living with His followers. Did

He teach them directly? Of course, but He also laughed with them, fished some late nights, and loved them as brothers.

In terms of personal evangelism, many modern believers take to one extreme or the other: Either (1) unloading the entire packaged gospel on complete strangers, or (2) defending their "lifestyle evangelism" void of direct mention of Jesus as sufficient.

Where have you fallen in this spectrum? Why?

Jesus lived in the middle. He lived as an example, and He spoke His faith out loud. His most successful disciples knew Him like family. His life was their ultimate education, in deliberate moments of teaching, in fellowship, and in observation.

Jesus told us exactly how to get started. After His resurrection, He appeared many times to His disciples to give them direct instructions on their mission. His very last words on this earth were, "But you will receive power when the Holy Spirit comes on you; and you will be my witnesses in

Jerusalem,
and in all Judea
and Samaria,
and to the ends of the earth" (Acts 1:8).

He said to begin in Jerusalem. Guess where they were? Jerusalem. In ascending order, He began with their city, then the entire region. He widened out and included the neighboring region, then cast a vision for the whole world. That would come as the mission expanded. But did you catch it? Begin where you are. Start in your own family, your neighborhood, your workplace. Who do you know? Who already knows you? What relationships have you already cultivated?

In your life, who needs Christ? Who is on your immediate list? List everybody you can think of in your family, workplace, circle of kids' friends, your hair stylist—if you know them and they don't know Jesus, write their names down.

As you live out your faith, it becomes time to share it. Listen Girls, that doesn't mean you present the 7-Step Roman Road to Salvation and pour oil on people's heads. You just include Jesus in conversation naturally. You give the reason for your joy. You mention your church and invite others to come along. Even better, you ask questions about what others believe. You listen without judgment. You love them and care for them supernaturally. Sometimes this occupies an entire conversation. Sometimes it takes two sentences. Almost always, it's ongoing.

Our mission doesn't fail if we don't get someone on her knees within eight minutes. Our goal is to intrigue someone, pique her hope just enough so she might lie in bed one night and whisper, "Jesus? Are you really there?" If we can help her to that point, He will answer. Jesus is a very compelling Savior.

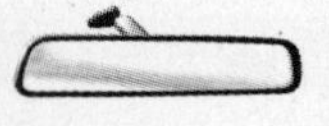

*What misconceptions about sharing your faith do you need to abandon?

Like the other aspects of discipleship, this is a road trip. We shouldn't sprint forward recklessly or stand still. Take one step: Ask a spiritual question of a coworker. Take another: Invite a neighbor to church. One more: Share briefly about how Jesus has replaced your despair with love. This is how our mission begins. God designed it to be self-propelling, because the moment you share your faith with someone who receives it, you will ache to share it with someone else.

Go on and try it.
Change your Jerusalem.
Together, we'll tackle the ends of the earth.

Will you be this full-circle disciple? Will you be obedient? Believe in Jesus' empowering spirit. Ask for the opportunities this week to talk about Christ to someone specific in your life.

DAY FIVE

Rest Stop

By the time we get to Peter's letters, he is a man among men. He has lived out his extraordinary faith for some forty-three years. Gone is the young, rash Peter. There is no hint of the scared Peter that denied his Friend three times. In fact, Peter became so highly regarded that Acts 5:15 tells us people tried to get close enough so his shadow might fall on them as he passed. As he wrote his letters in the final four years of his life, he had fulfilled his mission, making thousands of disciples on Jesus' behalf. What a disciple we have to learn from! *Love you, Peter!*

Let's pray through some of his writings. He knew better than anyone how to train disciples. He had a good Teacher. After each passage, spend a few minutes praying and journaling through your personal connection (feel free to use the prompts). Write your thoughts honestly and allow Jesus to stretch you as His disciple. It's okay to spend all your time in one or two passages. Quality counts more than quantity.

Accept your call with abandon, leaving your nets. Read 1 Peter 1:1-5.

- With believers around the world, you have been chosen! What have you been chosen for, according to verse 2?

Have you felt the intensity of that honor? Will you accept the worth He has esteemed you with by selecting you as a disciple?

- Has your life depicted a "new birth"? Has the old gone or have you tried to merge the two? The nets we hold onto will perish, spoil, and fade. What must you release?
- Will you instead follow Jesus as your living hope beginning today?

Immerse yourself in the example of Jesus, the Word made flesh. Read 1 Peter 1:13-16,23-25.

- Is your mind prepared for action by focusing on Jesus? How are you striving to be holy? What Jesus qualities do you need to imitate more?
- Are you plugged into the living Word of God? How does your relationship with Scripture need to grow? Only the Word will stand forever. What false pedestal have you tried to stand on?

Throw yourself headlong into the work and fellowship of the church. Read 1 Peter 4:8-11.

- Jesus said His true disciples would be known by their love for each other. What believer do you need to love on this week? Be reconciled to? How will you demonstrate Christ's love specifically?
- How has God's grace gifted you? How can you use that gift to serve your church? What steps will you take to obey?
- If you are in leadership already, check out 1 Peter 5:2-4.

Take on Jesus' mission and make new disciples for Him. Read 1 Peter 2:12; 3:15-16.

- What does your lifestyle look like to the unbelievers within your influence? Does it cause them to look favorably or spitefully at God? What needs to change?
- Do you give voice to the hope you have in Jesus? When you do, is it in gentleness or combativeness? Write out the answer you would give if someone asked you, "What's different about you?"

Spend time praying about your journey of discipleship. Ask boldly for the power of the Holy Spirit to deeply teach you about Jesus, enrich your gifts for use, and empower you to carry on Jesus' mission.

> "Come, follow me," Jesus said, "and I will make you fishers of men." (Matthew 4:19)

WEEK FIVE

Contentment

[Paul]

DAY ONE

Insatiable

I have this thing about working out. First of all, I hate it. I do it only under duress. I have a new layer of bonus flesh that is taking residence all over the top of my jeans. It has invited so many of its little fat-cell friends, they're beginning to spill over, and that's not pretty. So I halfheartedly work out whenever I can't find something better to do.

That's the truth.

So I'll confess to you that when someone in my circle gets all crazy and works out daily and starts to sound like an info-mercial personality in a size two, I do this thing. I launch into a few little rants that go something like:

> "What kind of person works out *every day*?"
> "Someone needs a job . . . "
> "Is it even pretty to be all toned?"
> "If thirty minutes of exercise a week isn't enough for you, then you're just obsessed."

Isn't that precious? Me thinks I doth protest too much. Anyone with a sliver of discernment can see through that tacky smokescreen. Who wants to have that kind of work ethic and the healthy body to match?

I do.

Discontentment manifests itself in many ugly ways. The results are nasty, but the root of the problem is even worse. Restlessness, dissatisfaction with ourselves, our lives, the season we're in, steals the very joy God intended to be our bread and butter.

*Before we get into it, do you struggle with discontentment? If so, in what areas?

Some women (I wouldn't know about it, but I'm told) think contentment means not wanting anything. Having no desires, no dreams, no passion. "Whatever you want is fine, Honey." If that rings any bells for you, talk about your want-free life.

Living a life of contentment involves embracing a series of steps that will revolutionize the way we exist. Our level of fulfillment informs every word we say and every decision we make. Contentment characterizes our victories, our middles, and our lowest lows. And since we always exist in one of those, it's a road worth our attention.

Paul is one of our best examples on this trip. He spoke uniquely to contentment, giving explicit instructions on how to obtain it. But before we get to that, let's take a look at Paul when he was still Saul. Just as the converted Paul was the picture of satisfaction, the murderous Saul was the epitome of discontent.

Here's what we know about Saul's background:

Read Acts 21:39. He was a Jew born in Tarsus, a wealthy city known for its great schools, rivaling those in Athens and Alexandria. It was a very cultured place to hail from. Tarsus was the capital city of the Roman province of Cilicia—which brings us to the next Saul fact.[1]

Read Acts 22:27-28. Saul had never set foot in Rome, yet he was a citizen of Rome. He didn't buy his citizenship or receive it as a reward (the other two ways to obtain it), but he was born into it. His family had gained citizenship at some point. That put Saul into an even more exclusive class. Roman citizens possessed a variety of legal protections, such as exclusion from all degrading forms of punishment.[2] Saul didn't know it, but someday that citizenship would come in handy.

Read Acts 22:2-3. He was born in Tarsus but was brought up in Jerusalem. When he was young, his family moved to the center of Judaism and raised him there. He became a disciple under the rabbi Gamaliel, probably the most honored rabbi of the first century. Gamaliel was so beloved and revered that he was the first to receive the title of "Rabban," higher than Rabbi or Master.[3] His wise intervention convinced the council of Jewish elders to release Peter and the other apostles rather than kill them for their teachings (see Acts 5:33-40).

Read Acts 23:6. Saul was a Pharisee, as was his father. He was a teacher in the synagogue and a religious example in the eyes of the people. He had authority in discernment and

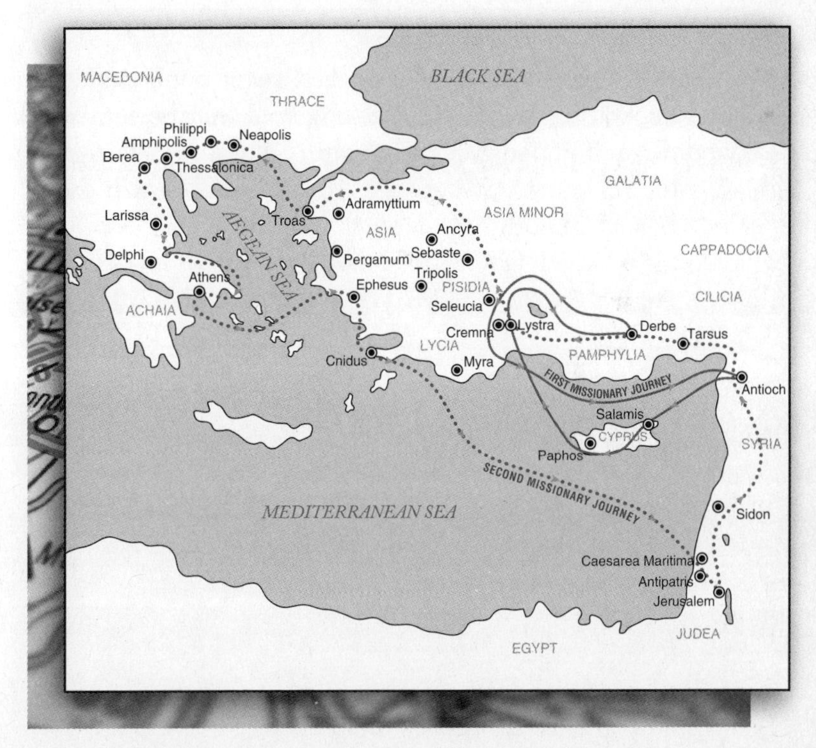

Paul's First and Second Missionary Journeys

Scripture. Other Jews admired Pharisees, as they were more "of the people" than the aristocratic Sadducees.

So what does this matter regarding contentment? Let's sum up Saul's pedigree:

- Born into the upper-middle class in a very class-conscious society
- Lifetime protection and privileges as a Roman citizen
- Chosen to study as a disciple of the most honored rabbi in Judaism
- Admired as a Pharisee, a select religious distinction

Separate yourself from what you know about Saul's later life. Just looking at his privileges, what kind of man would you expect him to be?

Despite his privileges, when we first meet Saul, he is the picture of a soul on fire with an aching void that burned with discontentment. His pedigree hadn't satisfied him or even curbed his appetite. Although an outsider would look at his life and conclude he lacked nothing—no material, emotional, or professional deficit whatsoever—he was actually a venomous black pit of discontent.

*Can you understand this discrepancy? What privileges or honors or status have you accrued that left you dissatisfied?

It is not coincidental that the first mention of Saul in Scripture is presented in stark contrast to the rich life of Stephen.

Read Acts 6:1-8. Why were Stephen and "the Seven" needed as leaders?

How would you describe Stephen?

Three times in this passage, Luke described Stephen with the same word: Full. Satisfied. Completed in Jesus. The Bible is silent on Stephen's material and social status, because they are completely irrelevant. In just a few verses we get a glimpse of his spirit, and it is wholly content—full of Christ and Christ alone.

You remember how I acted when faced with someone doing better than me? I didn't invent that defense mechanism, though it's probable I perfected it. Look what happened with Stephen.

Read Acts 6:9-15. What emotions did Stephen trigger in all these men?

The *New American Standard Bible* says, "they were unable to cope with the wisdom and the Spirit with which he was speaking" (verse 10). They simply could not take it. Worse yet, after all of their blustering and lying and false testimony, they looked over at Stephen, and he had the face of an angel. They fell apart. They couldn't shake his satisfied soul, *which wouldn't have mattered much if they were not so empty*.

Honestly, do you look at someone else with resentment because of his or her fullness? Can you dig deep and articulate what it is exactly that you're feeling?

Do you try to sabotage this person in any way? If so, how?

Look at the intense, almost painful manifestation of discontentment in the lives of these who brought false testimony against Stephen. As he stood strong and brought the truth of God boldly, their inner fires reached the boiling point.

Acts 7:2-53 records the speech Stephen gave about his faith to the city's council of leaders. How would you describe the leaders after that speech (see Acts 7:54-57)?

The more Stephen demonstrated his faith, the worse this situation escalated. Each new display of his strength pierced them deeper. The truth of his spiritual rightness brought their wrongness into such sharp relief that they were overcome with emptiness.

Read Acts 7:58–8:3. Forget Saul's pedigree. What do you see in him?

The Greek meaning behind the phrase "began to destroy" in Acts 8:3 was also used to describe the ravages of wild animals.[4] Do you see Saul now? If he wasn't aware of his deficit before, an hour spent in Stephen's presence left no room for doubt. And to soothe the agony of that encounter, to eliminate the truth that pierced him so deeply, he made it his mission to do away with every soul that knew Stephen's wholeness. Out of sight, out of mind.

Here is what strikes me: It is easy to reconcile the notion of discontentment to the unbelieving world. They don't know God. They're lost. Of course they're unfulfilled, and they don't even know why. That is clear and undisputed. But I believe the worst form of dissatisfaction belongs to *believers* who know just enough to know that life could be better, *should* be better.

But it's not.

That's certainly what we see in Paul. He had as much knowledge of God as was humanly possible to cram in. He had memorized the entire Hebrew Bible as an advanced student under Gamaliel. He'd read Moses' words of intimacy with God. He'd studied David's words of adoration. He'd seen a God who called his people "friends." He studied intensely what he didn't know personally. No wonder he was a mess. It would've been easier to be lost than know he didn't have what he could have.

*Does any of your discontentment come from knowing what a full, godly life could be but isn't in your experience? What do you feel like you're missing?

Oh Girls, there is hope! If contentment has been elusive for you, just think how far it was from Saul. He jailed and killed believers to quiet the storm within. He had everything, yet he had nothing. Like a ravaging animal, he tried to fill up on everything but Jesus. He tried so hard. He spiraled down from his good foundation until he was lost in darkness.

But Jesus found him.

How did Paul later articulate what God did for him (see 1 Timothy 1:12-17)?

*This passage makes me cry with love for our sweetest God. Why does God bear with us so?

Paul said he was once ignorant. Ignorance is simply *not knowing*. Unaware of God's satisfaction. Unaware of our spiritual privileges. Unaware of how to obtain the joyful life we hear about. Let me tell you some good news, Girls: God is patient with us in our ignorance. He understands how hard it is for us to wrap our finite arms around contentment that doesn't come from this world. And just like Paul, He will strengthen you, lavish you with abundant grace, and demonstrate His perfect patience if you are willing to risk finding contentment in Him alone.

A life lived in perfect satisfaction awaits you.

Our King has made it possible.

"Now to the King eternal, immortal, invisible, the only God, be honor and glory for ever and ever. Amen" (verse 17). Honor and glory to You, God. You are worthy. Amen and amen.

This journey requires a sacrifice. Will you lay down the temporary sources of contentment? Will you release the disappointments they brought? Ask God to prepare you for a paradigm shift this week. Godly satisfaction is a hard road, and it only has a few travelers. Pray for endurance and belief.

DAY TWO

Appetite

At first glance, contentment seems like a displaced topic in this study. The general message so far has been: Keep moving forward—don't be satisfied with the status quo of your spiritual life. There is more faith to practice, a better identity to embrace, a road of discipleship to travel. Go. Move. Grow. There's more. Then all of a sudden, I throw in contentment, which most of us would define as "be happy with what you have." It seems like we've down-shifted to a screeching halt.

What's up?

First of all, let's not confuse contentment with complacency. Being satisfied on a daily basis doesn't indicate a position or possession. It's not a destination. Many of us mistakenly assume that a certain season of life, a little more of this, or a little less of that will bring us to a place of contentment where we can put up our feet and finally be satisfied.

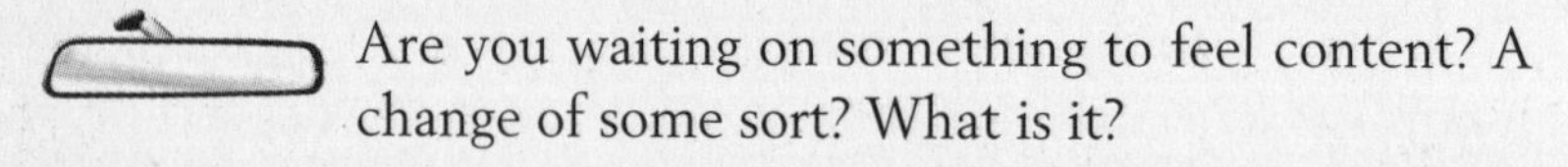

Are you waiting on something to feel content? A change of some sort? What is it?

Write a brief definition of what you think contentment means (don't try to be churchy or the teacher's pet—you won't be graded).

Secondly, many of us have misconstrued the meaning of contentment. It has been given a human slant, and the definition became distorted. If your definition described contentment as *happy where you are; having enough; needing nothing else*; or anything like that, I'll go ahead and give you a star. But if you will indulge me (like you have a choice), let's push through that standard definition of contentment and risk understanding it through a new lens.

Jesus gave us a radical notion of fulfillment: "Blessed are you who hunger now, for you will be satisfied" (Luke 6:21). What is so radical about that? Let's read closer. According to Jesus, contentment is distinguished not by finally having enough, but by being *constantly hungry*. In fact, what did He call the starving believer? Pathetic? Malnourished? Needy? No, Jesus called him "blessed." Our hunger for Christ has to be a permanent fixture.

So will God never fill us up? Will we always starve? Jesus used the word picture of "hunger" intentionally, so let's think of it in physical terms. You and I might sit down for breakfast at LeMadeline's and eat our weight in croissants. Super. You're a good friend candidate, and we're both stuffed. For the next five hours, we're golden. But guess what happens around one o'clock? *Rumble. Growl.* We'll have to meet at California Pizza Kitchen and eat again.

Contentment is perishable.

We will use up our supply.

Spiritually, it is designed to be a constant filling of a constant hunger.

*Why might God have planned it this way? List every reason you can think of.

So what does this mean for us? We can all relate to that appetite, the need to strive toward contentment. We starve for fulfillment, don't we? Solomon articulated it well in Proverbs 16:26: "The laborer's appetite works for him; his hunger drives him on."

As a whole, mankind is driven by hunger.

Girls, you will be filled by whatever you're hungry for. Contentment is not a matter of God being capable of satisfying us. His end of the deal is 100 percent guaranteed. He told us literally hundreds of times in Scripture that those who hunger for Him will be satisfied. Period. It's a nonnegotiable. The "filling up" is His job, and He has a decent résumé.

What this clearly demonstrates is this: If you don't have godly contentment, you aren't hungry for it. You are starved for something else, and it has left you spiritually malnourished.

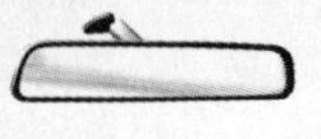

Where is your appetite driving you? What are you starved for? Money? Attention? Power? Validation? Status?

My appetite has wandered to the same junk food for years: approval. It has frequently tainted my offerings or spoiled a godly appointment. It has certainly distracted me from enjoying satisfaction from God because I was too busy trying to find it in the opinions of others.

I don't know what you hunger for. Collectively, our appetite for unhealthy things drives us into their arms, but they only offer partial fulfillment in return. We can all relate to that. There is one, and only one, source for complete contentment, and that's God. Girls, we need to *develop a hunger* for Him. That's our part. Let's let Him worry about satisfying it.

So how do we do that? Let's see what Paul did. His new appetite developed directly after his conversion. In its infancy, it grew larger and gained momentum, which prepared him for his calling. For the next two days, we're going to study Paul's satisfaction in Christ as it transcended circumstances, but let's take a quick look at how it began.

Paul's life took a radical turn when Jesus called and temporarily blinded him on the road to Damascus. He was on his way to lynch a few more Christians when Jesus waylaid him. In a brief conversation, he was transformed from Jesus' enemy into

His chosen instrument. This is the true power of Jesus, who can absolutely alter the trajectory of an entire life through one simple encounter. The King summoned Paul, and things would never be the same.

Read Acts 9:10-19. Put yourself in Saul's shoes. What is going through his mind on this day?

God does His part to jump-start a healthy hunger for righteousness. In your first moment of belief, the Holy Spirit takes full and instantaneous residence in your soul, just as He did with Saul (verse 17). He inhabits the hearts of His people, making daily guidance, conviction, and discernment immediately accessible. Learning to tap into the Spirit within you is the most certain way to develop a healthy hunger for Christ. If you submit to His constant presence, He will strengthen your appetite for God moment by moment. That's His function.

Read Acts 9:18-22. What evidence do you see of the powerful workings of the Holy Spirit?

Generally speaking, believers don't think about the Holy Spirit that much. We talk a lot about God and Jesus (which is fine, by the way), but the Spirit doesn't get much press. He's kind of an "idea." The Holy Spirit. . .whoooooooo. . .oogity boogity.

But the Spirit is pivotal. His inner presence revolutionizes life as a God-follower. The two purposes of Jesus' sacrificial death were to give us: (1) salvation through grace, and (2) the Holy Spirit—neither of which was universally available before. If you embrace one without the other, I'd venture to say your life is marked by discontent.

This feels a little tricky, doesn't it? I mean, what's up with the Holy Spirit? How are we supposed to live in the moment with Him? What does that even mean? I have some thoughts. First of all, acknowledge Him. He is a "He," not an "It." He is equal to the Father, equal to the Son. He is worthy of love and affection just as much as Jesus, who took our place on the cross. He has always been there, same as the other Two. Even in the Old Testament, God allowed the Spirit to be known selectively.

Isaiah reminded us of the Spirit's role with Moses and the Hebrews way back before Jesus:

> Where is he who set
> his Holy Spirit among them,
> who sent his glorious arm of power
> to be at Moses' right hand. . . .
> like cattle that go down to the plain,
> they were given rest by the Spirit of the LORD.
> This is how you guided your people
> to make for yourself a glorious name.
> (Isaiah 63:11-12,14)

This same presence, this same power, this same pillar of fire is the Holy Spirit in your very heart every single second of every single day, guiding you to contentment. Can you imagine? Acknowledge Him, Girls. Have a conversation with Him. Be real. What do you need to say to Him?

- I don't know You, but I want to. . . .
- I don't know how to hear You. . . .
- I'm not sure if what I'm hearing is You. . . .
- I only think of You when I need something. . . .
- Help me to feel Your presence. . . .

I have another thought. Quit ignoring Him. Oh, yes. That's what I said. If you believe, the Spirit moved into your heart, so it's not like He skipped you. He speaks to His beloved. You might recognize His voice as those pesky convictions you bat away. Those whispers that tug at the corners of your mind are usually His, too. "Don't do this." "Say that." "Love on this person." "Commit to this." "Don't commit to that." You know those? I sure do.

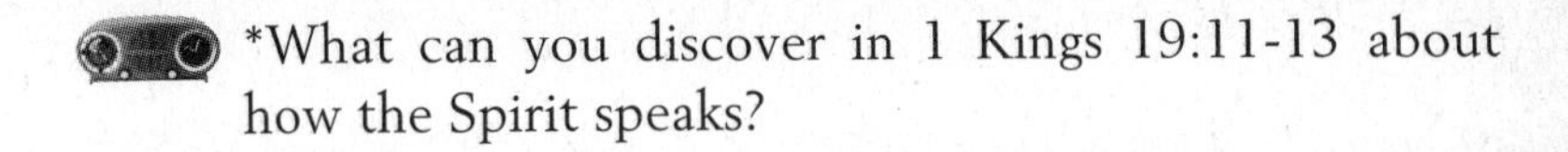

*What can you discover in 1 Kings 19:11-13 about how the Spirit speaks?

What gentle whispers have you been ignoring?

Girls, the first step in developing a healthy hunger for Christ is to become close friends with the Holy Spirit. He'll direct your appetite away from empty fillers and turn it instead to the fullness of God. He Himself is a spiritual fullness we can barely comprehend. This relationship alone is enough to keep you hungry for the things of Jesus until the day you die, but it is a *daily* endeavor.

1. Acknowledge Him for who He really is.
2. Quit ignoring the guidance of His whispers.
3. Invite Him to walk with you. Every. Single. Day.

The filling of the Holy Spirit enabled Paul to transform from a killer to a preacher in a matter of days. His misguided appetite was quickly redirected to the truth of Jesus Christ. His sin became surrender in the waters of baptism, his enemies became his brothers, and his stakeout became his sanctuary. I bet the whisper he heard in his ear was:

"My chosen son, you are redeemed. You are forgiven. You are loved. Let's get to work."

Do you need to embrace the whole benefit of salvation? Have a conversation with the Holy Spirit today. If you've left Him out, ask for forgiveness. Welcome His voice, and ask Him to develop your ear. Commit to beginning every single day with an invitation: "Spirit, walk with me; I'm listening."

DAY THREE

The Secret

For a few really fun years, I taught fourth grade. It was this great in-between grade where we could talk about important issues, but they still thought I was perfect. Sweet little fools. Now I certainly knew my audience. I remembered fourth grade all too well: Long, stringy hair occasionally fried by a home perm, horrific plastic glasses, grown-up horse teeth in a nine-year-old mouth, not a pair of Guess jeans to be found (thanks for nothing, Mom), painful awareness of every deficiency.

So on the first day of school each year I taught, I wanted to deliver a message that mattered to my students. I brought a suitcase full of "Mrs. Hatmaker stuff" and took out items piece by piece, explaining their significance in my life or my history. The grand finale was an 8x10 of my fourth-grade picture. You have never seen such shock and awe on thirty faces as they stared at that gawky, awkward image. They'd look at the picture. . . then at me. . . at the picture. . . back at me. Every year, the message was delivered loud and clear: Girls, don't despair—there is hope for you.

Paul was the master of delivering the right message to the right audience. Through the Spirit, he always knew exactly what they needed to hear. His most eloquent, profound teaching on contentment—both in action and written word—was delivered to the Philippians.

Why did they need to hear it?

Fourteen years after Paul's radical conversion, he set out on his first missionary journey with his friend, Barnabas. It lasted two years, and churches were planted in towns all over Pisidia and Galatia, in what is now Turkey (see map on page 129). The laborious work of bringing the gospel to the Gentiles had begun. A year later, Paul was itching to check on his fledgling churches.

Read Acts 15:36-40. After parting ways with Barnabas, who was Paul's new travel companion? (Acts 15:22,32 has more information about him.)

Early in the journey, who else did they pick up (see Acts 16:1-3)? What do you learn about him?

Before they went to Philippi, they picked up a fourth cohort in Troas. Read Acts 16:10. Notice the writer of Acts uses the term "we" from this point. Who wrote Acts?

This is the dream team: a Jewish Roman citizen, another full Jew from the center of Judaism, a half-Jew half-Greek, and a Gentile Christian. Don't you love God's handiwork? He'll take His message to whomever He wants through whomever He wants. Don't try to box Him in. God is not dictated by our contrived prejudices.

Now Luke told us in Acts 15:36 that Paul's intention was to revisit the churches he had started, give them a preachin' to, and encourage their progress. Like a proud Papa Bear coming to see his babies growing up. He *loved* these people. We know from his writings that he treasured these relationships. This was a reunion he couldn't even wait one year for.

But read Acts 16:6-8.

Hmmmm. He and his buddies got to Troas and joined up with his "dear friend Luke, the doctor" (Colossians 4:14). Troas was the last port city in Asia on the Mediterranean Sea. All that was left was to cross over to Macedonia, where the first stop was Philippi, in Europe (see map on page 129). What's up with this detour, God? What about my babies I was going to check on?

Just like Abraham, Paul obeyed the Spirit's leading to the maximum capacity. Once he proved faithful, God gave him further instructions.

Read Acts 16:9-10. Why do you think God led Paul through this particular vision rather than simply through promptings from the Holy Spirit as before?

Luke tells us they "immediately" hustled over to Philippi—a credit to Paul's zeal for Christ and the lost, not his own agenda. Once there, affection for this place quickly took root. Accustomed to teaching in synagogues, Paul was handed a new card here.

History tells us at least ten Jewish *men* were required to organize a synagogue. But there was no synagogue here, which tells us there weren't even ten Jewish men to piece one together.[5] He was truly a long way from home. Either by the directions of a Philippian or the leadership of the Spirit, the team found themselves outside city limits, gathered at the banks of the Gangites River.

Read Acts 16:11-15. What was God up to all this time?

*What does this tell you about Him?

This special place with such a unique calling for Paul's attention began with a bunch of girls! The first convert and the only Philippian mentioned by name in Acts was a savvy businesswoman! *This* was who God diverted Paul to! God chicks! Don't ever let anyone deceive you into thinking the church is a Boys' Club.

Now, why does this matter? Let's go full circle. Remember how we talked about Paul's gift for pegging the right message for the right audience? We now know the church at Philippi began with women. We also know that women continued to carry the load of this church, alongside men, because ten years later Paul wrote urging two women to reconcile (Philippians 4:2-3). Though calling them out on a disagreement, he commended "these women who have contended at my side in the cause of the gospel."

Guess what the theme of Paul's letter to this girl-filled church was?

Contentment.

Oh Girls, God's got our number.

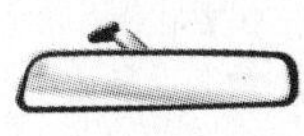

*In what ways do women have a unique struggle with contentment?

God took great pains to get Paul to His girls in Philippi, and then inspired an entire letter on the subject for us future girls. Paul wrote to the Philippians ten years after beginning the church, while he was under house arrest in Rome. Not surprisingly, this church had financially supported Paul ever since Paul's team left them. Women are famous for generosity. Much of Philippians is Paul's gratitude for their consistent support, but laced all throughout is a direct message on contentment.

Read Philippians 4:10-12. What does Paul suggest we are prone to base our contentment on?

*How have your circumstances affected your faith?

Paul says specifically, "I have *learned* to be content whatever the circumstances" (verse 11). In fact, he goes on to say he learned *the secret* of being content. Oh, please tell us, Paul! For almost thirty years you've been beaten, jailed, threatened, abandoned, lost at sea, shipwrecked, bitten by a viper, and you're now in chains. Your life is a train wreck as far as we can tell. We're pretty sure you should hook up with Job's wife, who tells

Job to "curse God and die" (Job 2:9). You obviously have the secret we need to hear. Tell us.

He drops it in Philippians 4:13. Why do you think Paul describes this as a secret?

Paul learned this secret not at the feet of Gamaliel, but at the feet of Jesus. Here is a fact: As long as you are trying to obtain contentment by your own methods, you will never be satisfied. If you are solely responsible for defining your dreams, making them happen, and managing the disappointments, you will become insatiable, as Paul well understood.

Contentment is supernatural. You know it is. It is the most unnatural quality I can think of. What is less natural than being content in need? Who can obtain that out of sheer willpower? I can't. You can't. I'm sure we've both tried and found it an exercise in futility.

We love Philippians 4:13, and we quote it all the time. But in context, it was written specifically toward *gaining contentment*. It might have been written: I can enjoy contentment in all things through Him who gives me the strength to do so. We're in luck—it's mostly out of our hands.

Except for this: We must hunger for it. Remember: Contentment is not a matter of being full; it's a matter of being hungry. Asking Jesus daily for His satisfaction is part of that spiritual hunger we must maintain. Most of us drowning in discontent are fully attempting to fill the holes ourselves. We're trying harder, working more, making grander plans. Paul had his eye on Jesus, and he wanted for nothing when we'd say he lacked everything.

In fact, while he was still in Philippi, he and Silas were severely beaten and jailed for commanding an evil spirit out of a girl whose possession was turning a profit for her fortune-telling masters (see Acts 16:16-24). His response both set an example for the women of his new church and tapped into the secret of contentment in any circumstance.

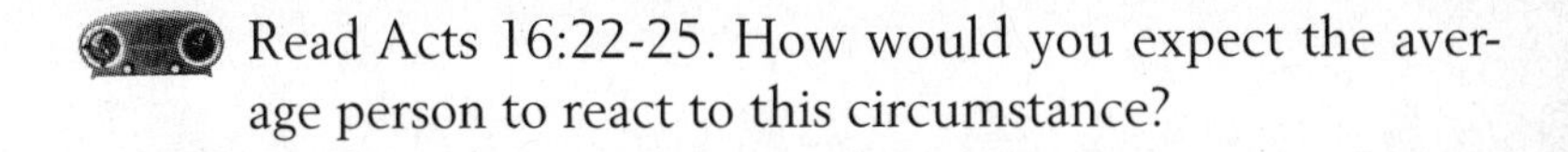 Read Acts 16:22-25. How would you expect the average person to react to this circumstance?

What secret did Paul and Silas demonstrate? How?

*Taking our focus from circumstances to the worship of God is a powerful weapon against discontentment. It activates God's strength to supernaturally administer peace. Consider your most challenging circumstance right now. List five reasons to praise Jesus either in spite of it or because of it.

Does this mean Paul and Silas weren't scared? Does contentment render us void of emotion while in need? Certainly not. There is a time to weep (see Ecclesiastes 3:4). Don't mistake satisfaction in Christ for being numb to real feelings. But Paul and Silas hungered to praise God more than to feel good. They worshiped *through* their fear, knowing God had called them to this place, knowing their praise would lead to the salvation of others, knowing God would strengthen them as He had many times before. They hungered for their Father, and He satisfied them in their chains (see Philippians 1:12-14).

Contentment is that underscoring security that holds you fast when the ground beneath your feet falls out. It is saying, "I'm Your child" in the *midst* of fear. It is searching out Jesus even though everything else is a question mark. It is sacrificially laying down your dissatisfaction and replacing it with gratitude. Contentment looks to heaven in worship, lifting up God, knowing He will also lift you up in your need. It stops you from throwing up your hands and declaring yourself abandoned.

You *can* be satisfied in tears. You *can* find contentment through disappointments. Your spirit *can* feel full in the midst of need. This is a gift from God, who has made a way for us to endure this world while we wait for our heavenly citizenship. Jesus offers satisfaction in want, when our deficiencies threaten to overwhelm us; in plenty, when our abundance can inflame our greed; and in suffering, when our losses urge us to despair.

Girls, let's worship at the feet of Jesus and learn the secret of contentment. We can know satisfaction in *everything* through Him who gives us strength.

Have you allowed yourselves to be tossed about by circumstances? What circumstance inhibits your contentment right now? Spend time today praising God for this situation, and find Him in the details. Allow worship to ignite contentment.

DAY FOUR

Ravenous

I have Girlfriends who are extremely in tune with their bodies. They recognize every little change. Symptoms are identified way before they progress to "I'm so sick, I need my mother." They would never have entered the ninth week of their first pregnancy before they realized something was amiss. (Guilty.) They even go to the gynecologist's office *once a year*. I call that obsession, but whatever.

I am not in my Girlfriends' club. I don't pay attention to anything that is going on internally unless it involves a fetus. And since that ship has sailed, it is likely I could develop any number of internal diseases and be none the wiser for it. I'd probably just be happy I was losing weight without trying and chalk it up to good karma.

Except for this one exception: I am laser focused when it comes to hunger. All activities come to an abrupt halt when I hear a growl. Let's be honest: I don't even have to hear a growl. In fact, I always look in shock at my Girlfriends who say, "I just forgot to eat." Huh? How are we even friends? I forgot to put shoes on my kids? Maybe. I forgot to give my husband my weekly receipts? Definitely. I forgot to eat? Never.

So it is with great enthusiasm that I enter today's writing. Today I teach on hunger, and I'm a specialist. It is literally the only thing I can articulate about my own body.

So far, we've defined contentment not as having enough, but being constantly hungry for Christ. Rather than striving for fullness, we strive for hunger. That is our goal. God handles the daily filling. How, then, do we develop this hunger?

Glad you asked. I really know this (and so did Paul). Let's talk about two surefire ways to become ravenous.

1. Dieting

If there is a quicker way to make your stomach threaten to implode from agony, I haven't found it. I've only been on a diet a total of maybe thirty days in my whole life (because I am a fan of eating), but I know for sure that when the sugar, white fluffy carbs, fried delicacies, and butter get cut in favor of things that are green and leafy and appropriately portioned, I feel as if I live in a third-world country. I'm hungry all blasted day long.

A healthy spiritual diet will amp up your hunger for Christ with the same intensity. There are so many unhealthy choices that temporarily fill us and leave us bloated. To begin a fast from the junk will increase our hunger for what makes us fit.

Today we're going to take a look at some great advice Paul gave young Timothy as he led the church Paul planted in Ephesus. He spoke to one of the greatest enemies of contentment in terms of an unhealthy diet.

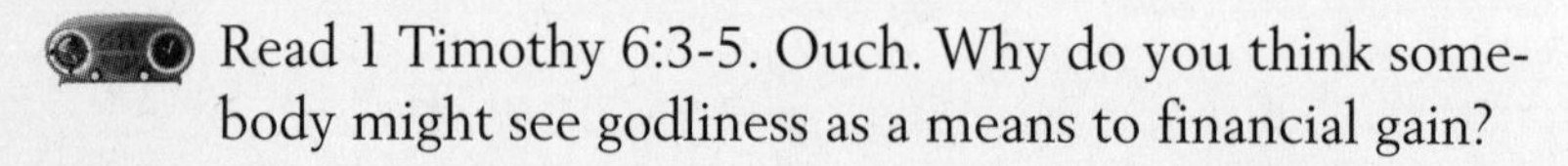

Read 1 Timothy 6:3-5. Ouch. Why do you think somebody might see godliness as a means to financial gain?

*How did this misunderstanding impede contentment in their lives?

Because our culture equates contentment with financial gain, it is extremely difficult to separate ourselves from this view. We feast on possessions—a bigger house, a nicer car—and the accolades that come from owning our beautiful things. For girls especially, this often consumes our diet. It seems like the avenue to fullness. If we can acquire enough, we'll be satisfied, and we'll have successfully kept up with the Joneses.

How do you struggle with the desire for material possessions?

What typically stimulates your desire? (For instance, you see people on television with something. Or you see your friend has something. Or you see something while window shopping. And what goes through your mind is . . .)

Paul spoke the truth about true fulfillment, true gain. Remember, he knew what he was talking about. He came from money and prestige, but he was writing from prison. He had truly walked on both sides of the material tracks. He had fully experienced possessions. He had fully experienced poverty.

His informed conclusion is in 1 Timothy 6:6-10. What are the dangers of the love of money?

*How do you respond to Paul's idea of being content merely with food and clothing? Why?

Girls, do you need to fast from a love of money and the things it buys? Look deep down. Money in and of itself is not the problem for Paul. In fact, God gave abundant financial resources to people throughout history to be used for His kingdom, for the poor, to accomplish his work. But *money* and the *love of money* are two different things. One can be used in healthy stewardship and generosity, while the other becomes a temptation, a trap, a piercing grief.

What financial or material temptation do you need to eliminate from your diet?

Once this filler is eliminated, you will be shocked at your capacity for spiritual hunger. The deceptive blinders come off, and you'll see the healthy things of Christ with the same voracity you once viewed possessions. With your hunger appropriately directed, you'll finally know satisfaction. "Godliness with contentment is great gain" (verse 6).

2. Exercising

In order to make it more palatable, my Girlfriends and I exercise together. We run on the treadmill side by side at the gym or walk at our beautiful Town Lake here in Austin. My Girlfriend Trina and I just took a step class together for the first time, and we were the only two people who consistently had no idea what we were doing. This is why we go together. One equals humiliation. Two equals hilarious.

But then we do a funny thing. Because the physiology of exercising creates an unmatched hunger, our reward for our sacrificial training is always. . . food. Exercising gives us the right to eat a fried chicken sandwich at Chick-Fil-A. Counterproductive? Let's call it a gray area.

Physical exertion results in intense hunger and thirst. Spiritual exertion has the same effect. One surefire way to develop a hunger for Christ is to get busy doing His work. Paul frequently spoke about the similarities between our physical and spiritual bodies. Again, Paul instructed Timothy on how to exercise his spirit:

*Read 1 Timothy 4:7-10. How is it possible to "train yourself to be godly" (verse 7)? How is that like physical training?

If you want to develop a hunger for God, begin taking part in His labor. Paul told Tim that our God-work ultimately results in spiritual health. Even if it feels sluggish at first, your metabolism for "true gain" will quickly speed up. On the contrary, lying around doing nothing for the kingdom slows down your metabolism for godliness to a crawl. This doesn't mean you aren't busy; it means you aren't busy for God.

 What work for God's kingdom do you take part in? If the answer is none, why is that?

Paul gave Timothy some great specifics in 4:11-15. How might Timothy's obedience in these matters have fueled his young hunger for Christ?

What if you're not gifted in preaching and teaching? What are some other ways to exercise your spiritual muscles?

What is amazing about working for God is the unexpected payoff. Just like exercising, the more you work, the stronger you get. The more you see the fruits of your labor, the more you want to work. Your spiritual metabolism speeds up exponentially. God is just that smart to come up with a cycle that both accomplishes His work and nourishes the worker at the exact same time. Laboring for Him definitely intensifies your hunger for Christ, and the deeper your hunger, the deeper your satisfaction when God fills it with His healthy blessings.

Contentment definitely requires a sacrifice of familiar nourishment. It means laying down our unhealthy diets and abandoning our comfortable complacency. But the hardest work is on the front end when it is a leap of faith. God immediately fulfills His end of the bargain by lavishing us with satisfaction and wholeness. Once you start down the road of godly hunger, you are immediately met with the nourishment you need to travel on: godly contentment.

True gain.

I never thought I'd say this, but starvation rocks.

Will you commit to developing your hunger for God? Ask Him to show you what you need to fast from. Replace those false fillers with healthy replacements: God's Word, Christian fellowship, a strong work ethic for eternal tasks. Will you take this leap of faith and trust that God will fill you with true contentment?

DAY FIVE

Rest Stop

Paul is such a beautiful example of a man who constantly starved for Christ. Jesus came as our Savior; Paul showed us how to live for Him. His model is worth our attention. Let's pray and journal through one of Paul's most profound passages: Philippians 3:4-11. It exemplifies his hunger for Christ and, consequently, his contentment. Feel free to use the prompts, or allow the Spirit to lead you through the verses on your own.

Read Philippians 3:4-6. This used to be Paul's banquet table. He feasted on his pedigree, his privileges, and his positions. They were the sources of his false confidence.

- Consider the menu on your banquet table of satisfaction. What do you feast on? What engorges you? Journal through your history and current position just like Paul did. Be honest.
- Do you need to clear the entire table and start over? Or maybe just pick a couple of unhealthy items off (see examples below)? List three to five ways you can fast from your unhealthy power sources. How will you devalue their influence over your state of contentment?

- Financial gain: Fast from any mention of money or possessions for two weeks, don't spend money on anything but necessities for a period, focus your attention on giving or on someone who has less than you, not more.
- Attention: Pick one person a day to focus on other than yourself. Change the avenues by which you gain attention (the way you dress, the words you say).

Read Philippians 3:7-9. Here we see the extent of Paul's hunger for Christ and the depth to which God has satisfied his appetite. This is our goal, Girls.

- In the previous section, you identified your areas of necessary "loss," which Paul speaks of three times. Write briefly to God about how you truly feel about losing those comforts. It's okay to be honest. God can handle your fears.
- Now Paul identifies the "gains" that come from being satisfied in Christ alone. In other words, this is what contentment looks like. Journal about each of the following gains. If you have time, look up the cross-reference and briefly journal on the connection that jumps out at you:
  - "The surpassing greatness of knowing Christ Jesus my Lord" (verse 8). See also John 10:14-16.
  - To "gain Christ and be found in Him" (verses 8-9). See also 1 Peter 1:2-3.
  - "The righteousness that comes from God" (verse 9). See also Romans 3:10 and 2 Timothy 4:8.

How do you feel about these gains? How do they compare to your losses?

Read Philippians 3:10-11. To me, this is the crescendo. I can see Paul in his chains, very aware of his immense losses, yet declaring, "I just want to know Christ." Truly, he considered everything else rubbish. This "knowing" is not simply academic. In fact, Paul goes on to describe this knowledge of Jesus as *experiential.* Really knowing Jesus must extend well beyond the boundaries of information.

- How can you know the power of Jesus' resurrection? What does that mean to you? How does this transition from "the knowledge of Jesus' resurrection" to "the power of Jesus' resurrection"? How does this equate to *really* knowing Jesus? Write out everything that comes to mind.
- How about knowing Jesus by sharing in His sufferings? What do you suffer right now on His behalf? Nothing? In living a life of hunger for Him, what might you suffer for His name pretty quickly? Would a relationship have to be redefined? Would your time have to be reallocated? How would this increase your knowledge of Jesus? Write through these questions.

Close by writing out one or two verses that uniquely connected with you today. Write them as a prayer. If you don't feel this way yet, write them as a request. Spend some time in prayer thanking Jesus for the "gains" He made available to you. Pray them out loud in praise.

WEEK SIX

Service

(The Church)

DAY ONE

The Estate

When I first received my driver's license, I figured I had arrived. Not only was I a *legal* threat now, but my parents gave me my own car. Admittedly, it was a piece. It was a 1979 Chevette in which, perhaps, half of everything worked. But it was mine, and I could drive it anywhere. I was a child of freedom. Or so went my line of thinking.

A few bumps in the road of driving bliss soon raised their ugly little heads. Bumps such as:

- Jen, drive your sister to her friend's house.
- Jen, pick up your sister from her friend's house.
- Jen, go buy your own tampons (when Ty Miller, the hottest senior ever, was working the only checkout lane). Horror.
- Jen, try to understand that when your car runs out of gas, you must fill it or it will discontinue running.
- Jen, try to understand that since your car is a diesel, "regular unleaded" is a bad choice.

Who knew? I just wanted to drive around town and be as cool as my car would allow me to be, but what was with all that responsibility? What a pain! What a cramp in my obvious style! After filling my tank with a portable gas container on the side of the road—again—my Dad finally had to say the words: "With privilege comes responsibility. You can't have one without the other."

Touché.

This could also be our spiritual mantra. Take a look at our privileges: They are so numerous I'd max out my remaining word count mentioning them all. So let's hit a couple of highlights.

What benefits do the following Scriptures promise you?

Psalm 103:2-5

Romans 6:20-22

Not bad. That's the VIP treatment if I ever saw it. Is there literally one more thing we could possibly ask for that isn't covered in our fringe benefits? We are privileged indeed.

If these are our benefits, let's consider our Employer. Imagine God's kingdom as a massive, multi-zillion-dollar estate covering millions of acres. It exports to every country in the world. It is constantly growing, adapting, making new acquisitions. The amount of man hours necessary to maintain productivity is untold.

So to staff His estate, He bypasses the Ivy-Leaguers and instead plucks the hopeless out of the gutter. He takes those who had nothing and gives them a brand new life. He chose you, cleaned you up, and brought you to His magnificent estate, where you are afforded the most comprehensive benefits available. In exchange, you are trained and equipped to help manage His sprawling domain. Now this is an extremely basic metaphor, but it's a Bible study, not a novel.

So try to imagine what it's like for the Boss to circulate through his enormous estate, barely able to keep up with the demand. He sees some employees diligently working overtime. They are passionate about their work, grateful for the opportunity to give back. In fact, many of them are doing the work of others in addition to their load. Then He rounds a corner and sees countless employees lounging around, wasting day after day—but still cashing in those paychecks every month. They're enjoying the benefits without logging any hours toward the success of the estate. How do you think this makes Him feel as such a generous benefactor?

Girls, with privilege comes responsibility. We shouldn't try to bankroll one while neglecting the other. We embrace salvation, we love forgiveness, we sleep at night knowing our eternity is secure. So what is our response? It seems obvious, yet 20 percent of God's people do 80 percent of His work.

*Here's how Jesus put it. Read Luke 17:7-10. How would you put into your own words the misguided attitude Jesus is addressing?

In what sense are we "unworthy servants" (verse 10)? Unworthy of what?

We would never take advantage of an earthly authority in such a crazy manner. We'd fall all over ourselves to work diligently if for no other reason than the fear of getting fired. To say nothing of *respect* or *gratitude*, which are the real things any sane Christian feels toward God. Can we really rationalize lazing around, presuming on the assurance that God loves us too much to fire us?

If an earthly boss gave us riches beyond measure with a simple request—"I need you to work hard for me"—you better believe we would. So why don't we treat God's generosity with the same tangible response?

I believe two major flaws keep most believers sidelined. First, we are utterly self-absorbed. "Me" takes precedence over "Other" nine times out of ten. We're wholly concerned about our agendas, our gains, our schedules, our comforts, our needs. Real perspective is hard to come by.

This keeps us out of service in two obvious ways. Some of us have simply left no room for God's business. We've stacked our schedules with the "vital" elements, leaving no time or energy for service to

God's kingdom. The very idea of rolling up our sleeves and getting down to serious God-work is exhausting to even think about.

Are you spent on temporary (that is, non-eternal) work? If so, what does your time go to?

Self-absorption can hinder God's work in another way, too. Consider this inner voice: *What do you think you could even do? You're not good enough to serve. That's for people who have it all together. You don't know enough. You haven't been at this long enough. You'll ruin the church.*

When focused inwardly, we get deceived into thinking serving is all about us. That's the flip side of self-absorption. We assume it depends on our merits, and we rob God of the opportunity to equip us and use us.

*Does this ring true? If so, how has negative self-absorption kept you out of the game?

The second attitude that keeps believers out of God's work is the loss of reverence. We are simply not all that impressed with God anymore. We're Americans! We pulled ourselves up by the bootstraps, and look at us now! We're rich! We're privileged! We're living the dream! Our raging successes as a country—brought by the deliverance of God, I'll remind you—have rendered us void of humility.

Our country reminds me of various stages in Israel's journey when God's hand was heavily upon them in blessings. He subdued their enemies, He enriched their bounty. He granted them worldwide favor. And what did they do every time? Abandoned reverence for pride, worship for pleasure. The very privileges God lavished them with became their downfall.

There was a time when God's name was considered so sacred that His people wouldn't even say it out loud. Only the high priest could utter "YHWH," and only once a year in the prayer of the Day of Atonement.[1] By contrast, we use God's name as a punch line, sometimes even a curse.

The Bible is always good for a little perspective. Read what Jesus taught in Luke 12:35-40. What attitudes and habits does He warn against?

If Jesus returned today, what kind of servant would He find in you? What makes you say that?

Just in case this passage has tricked you into thinking Jesus is really mean, let me say this: He is not being ugly. He is being urgent. Sometimes we need a helping of straight talk to get us off high center, and Jesus knows time is fleeting. Every day we are closer to His return. Every passing hour is a demonstration of His patience as He grants another chance to turn to Him (see 2 Peter 3:9). He is counting on us to make the most of this precious gift called time.

According to Luke 12:35-40, what is the Master's main attitude toward His *faithful* servants when He returns?

Right now, we are managers of God's estate. We are His servants, plain and simple. There is more work to be done than is humanly possible, so we have to rely on our Master's strength. We've been given unmatched privileges in this life and the one to come, and our only responsibility is to respond in gratitude and service. We will explore this journey in depth this week.

There will come a day, though, when we'll sit at the banquet table with our beloved Savior and feast side by side with Him. And after you've done your job and I've done mine, we'll hear the words He has saved for His dearest:

> "Well done, good and faithful servant! You have been faithful with a few things; I will put you in charge of many things. Come and share your master's happiness!" (Matthew 25:21)

"Pull up a chair."—Jesus

It's time to get busy. What do you need to confess today? Ask God to shine His light on the parts of your heart that need to bend to His workload. Ask Him how to get ready to serve Him the way He wants. Pray for wisdom this week as you discover your niche.

DAY TWO

Holy Fire

Alright, Girls, let's back up a bit and gain a little perspective on our road trip of service. We'll go way beyond the simple divisions of "privilege" and "responsibility." In fact, watch how our responsibility to serve God is actually just another line item on His privilege list.

Here we go: Before there was the church, there was the synagogue. This was the local meeting place of Jews. It wasn't the same thing as the temple. That was the Big Daddy worship facility with all the pomp and circumstance. The synagogue was small and simple, like a meeting hall. In Jesus' day, there were no fewer than 480 synagogues in Jerusalem. Rabbis taught school there throughout the week, and on the Sabbath, a five-part service was conducted, including prayers, psalm-singing, blessings, Scripture readings, and commentaries.[2]

I don't know about you, but this sounds pretty familiar. This isn't at all unlike the way we do church today. Granted, women sat in a separate section and couldn't take active part in the service then, but it was an intimate setting to learn and worship together. Good. Grand.

Here's the difference: The responsibilities of the synagogue pre-Jesus fell to a tiny minority. The head of the synagogue presided over the service and appointed teachers (see Acts 13:15).

His duties were largely administrative. Then there was the synagogue attendant, who cared for the building and assisted in the service as needed (see Luke 4:20). Finally, there were the rabbis, who brought the message. The end. That was the OT church. Everyone else just came and sat.

Why might Jesus have wanted to revolutionize this narrow arrangement?

Remember what Jesus taught his disciples in Caesarea-Philippi (Matthew 16:18)? "On this rock"—a confession of faith like Peter's—"I *will* build my church." The synagogue organization was about to change. Of course, they had no idea what that meant. The synagogue was all they knew. The new church wouldn't be realized until after Jesus was gone. Not because He didn't have the power to launch it, but because that role had been appointed to another.

Jesus told His disciples, "I tell you the truth: It is for your good that I am going away. Unless I go away, the Counselor will not come to you; but if I go, I will send him to you" (John 16:7). The launch of the church belonged to the Holy Spirit, and did He ever make a grand display. Jesus died on a Friday. The next day was the Passover Sabbath. Forty days later, He ascended into heaven (see Acts 1:9). Ten days after His ascension was Pentecost, the second most important Jewish celebration. It was one of three occasions when all men from every region were supposed to journey to the temple in Jerusalem for worship.[3]

Only fifty days removed from Jesus' crucifixion and resurrection, what would you expect to be the emotional and spiritual state of His followers? (You could look at Acts 1:13-14, which describes the previous ten days.)

Read Acts 2:1-13. Why do you think the Holy Spirit chose this moment to pour out His presence?

My Bible lists as the heading for this passage: Birthday of the Church. But this doesn't feel like a birthday. This feels like the floor of the stock market exchange on a bad acid trip. Where is the church in all this? Or as the Jews cried out, "What does this mean?" Bless 'em. They freaked out, and I'm not casting any stones, as I haven't been privy to many tongues of fire hovering over people's heads. Well, let's turn the page.

Here comes Peter. Jesus forgave him for pretending he didn't know Him when the heat was on. Peter was a new man. Read his speech in Acts 2:14-36. What was the new message of the church?

Why were the people "cut to the heart" (Acts 2:37)?

Here's the best part: Read Acts 2:38-47.

They started having them some church! *This* is what church looks like through the power of the Spirit! What's not to love, I ask you? I *so* feel this way about church. Brothers and sisters I love dearly, people who take great pains to care for each other, a place where Jesus' name is lifted high. We have the privilege of taking ownership in this magnificent movement! Serving here is nothing short of pure joy. When I read Acts 2, I am fully connected to my forerunners. I feel their excitement, and I cannot help but nod and share the love.

I'm not the only one who applauded. Check out what happened in the following months.

What happened to the church in each of the following passages?

Acts 4:4

Acts 5:14

Acts 6:7

Acts 9:31

Acts 9:35

Acts 9:42

Acts 11:19-21

Are you getting the picture? This new kind of church spread like wild fire! Not just to Jews in Jerusalem either—women, Greeks, Gentiles, Romans, Egyptians. . . Americans. Oh yes, the church reached over culture, time, persecution, distance. It's stronger today than it has ever been. *That* is the power of the Holy Spirit. What He ordained, let no man come against.

*How do you view the church? (For instance, to what extent do you see it as a flawed, man-driven entity, and to what extent as God's hand of mercy stretched out to every nation?)

How has your view affected your involvement?

Oh yeah, God ordained one more thing. As you can see, this is a giant estate. No longer do the responsibilities of the church rest in the hands of a few leaders. *Every* member gets to roll up her sleeves and dig in to grow this thing even stronger and broader. It's a fantastic new day. We are the blessed NT church, and we should *never* imitate the OT model of "come and sit."

The Spirit who started this church is the same Spirit who enables it to carry on. Here's how: "There are different kinds of gifts, but the same Spirit. There are different kinds of service, but the same Lord. There are different kinds of working, but the same God works all of them in all men. Now to *each one* the manifestation of the Spirit is given for the common good" (1 Corinthians 12:4-7).

Brilliant. This is how the Holy Spirit keeps His church in healthy working order. You are gifted. I am gifted. We're equipped differently to fill different needs, but if you are a believer, the Holy Spirit has blessed you with something unique. Something valuable. Something to serve His church with. Let's set out to find the gift we have to offer our Master. He's given us the privilege of responsibility.

I can hear the holy roar of the Spirit coming.

Are you a NT believer following the OT model? Do you need to pick up a new resolve? Pray for discernment as you investigate your spiritual gift tomorrow.

DAY THREE

The Circle of the Gifted

My oldest son, Gavin, is completely laser-focused on one thing at a time to the detriment of any activity around him. If I had harnessed this quality earlier, we could've stuck a Gameboy in his hands and administered his inoculations without having to hold him down like a deranged mental patient.

More times than I can count, I've asked him to do something while he's engrossed in something else. Told him. Told him again. Again. Then maybe I accidentally yelled at the top of my lungs one final time. Volume seems to be the only trump card. (I can hear the parenting experts groan.)

At this point, Gavin drops whatever he's doing and runs around in fast, spastic circles trying desperately to figure out what he is supposed to be doing. He heard yelling coupled with his name, but in terms of specifics, he's clueless. It's as if movement substitutes for obedience until—if there is a God—his mom says it one last time and he actually hears it.

This might be where some of us are today with service. We read the last two days, "*Get busy!*" and maybe we jumped up and ran in spastic circles with no earthly idea of what it is we're supposed to do. I want to be doing it! I'm a good little servant!

Running . . . Running . . . Looking around . . . Is there something right near me that will give me a clue?

Where are you right now with regard to service? (Does running around in spastic circles sound like you? What about sitting paralyzed or collapsed with exhaustion?)

There's good news: God has a plan. There won't be some weird mix-up that lands you at the pulpit next week preaching for your pastor (unless your name is Jen Hatmaker, and even then you'll be called a "guest speaker"), but I digress.

God's a smart one. He planned for His church, sent Jesus to revolutionize the landscape, and ignited it through the Spirit. The Trinity worked really hard for this one. So don't think for a second He forgot to tell us how to manage it. We have explicit directions in the Word on how to serve. Let's begin where we left off yesterday.

We throw the phrase "spiritual gifts" around a lot these days. Many Girlfriends have told me what a polarizing term that is when you have no idea of what to make of it. What's even up with that? Did someone make that up? Yes. God did.

Go back to 1 Corinthians 12:4-7. Can you tell from Paul's instruction what problems might have surfaced in the Corinthian church in terms of spiritual gifts? Write about what you see.

Matthew Henry wrote, "Spiritual gifts are bestowed, that men may with them profit the church and promote Christianity. They are not given for show, but for service; not for pomp and ostentation, but for edification; not to magnify those that have them, but to edify others."[4]

As individuals, the Corinthians were very gifted and experienced the Spirit in a special way (see 1 Corinthians 1:4-7). Yeah, God! But powerful gifts have a way of spoiling the child, don't they? The Corinthians quickly categorized gifts in descending levels and turned that into a pecking order of status in the church.

Do you treat some gifts displayed in your church as more important or being of a higher status than others? If so, which ones?

Perhaps unconsciously, how has this perception affected your own use of your gifts?

All too often, those with the conspicuous, publicly displayed gifts devalue the modest gifts. At the same time, those whose gifts keep them behind the scenes look at the preachers and teachers either in envy, bitterness, or insecurity. This makes a mess of things. Paul addressed it.

*Read 1 Corinthians 12:14-20. Are you a fully functioning part of your church body, or more like a detached limb? Why?

Sweetest Girls, you are so valuable. We have many special gifts because of the makeup of our personalities. God stamped wonderful qualities into women's hearts. Without making categories like the Corinthians, let me just say that we have some of the very best gifts. (Oops. I went ahead and did it.) Usually, it isn't other believers who look down on someone's gifts. It's the gifted one looking down on herself. Let's put that to bed.

Let's peek at some of the gifts of the Spirit. List the gifts described in the following passages. Note the overlaps and differences. Circle any gifts whose meaning you're not sure of.

1 Corinthians 12:8-10

Romans 12:6-8

Ephesians 4:11-12

Look at that! This is a church! What a bunch of winners! Can you imagine if the body of Christ willingly used all those gifts on a daily basis? Needs would be met. Love would be constantly distributed. Discipleship would be rich. Hearts would be strengthened. Can you imagine? God did. I told you He had a plan, and you're looking at it.

*Collectively, what do these gifts tell you about God?

Paul constantly said the Spirit distributed gifts according to His good will. He picked the right gift for the right believer every time. It wasn't a roll of the dice. It wasn't arbitrary. It was deliberate. It's important to understand His intentionality; otherwise, discovering our gifts would be like trying to find the one pair of size eight Jimmy Choos in a sea of bargain shoes. (That's a Girlfriend's take on "a needle in a haystack." I don't really know anyone who owns a pair of Jimmy Choos. I just see them on Oprah.)

If we understand that the Spirit matches us up with the perfect gift to serve His church, then there are some great clues we can look at to discover our niche. Since He knows us intimately, let's look at some of the same indicators He probably uses in the distribution process.

How would you describe your basic personality? (Introverted—you get more done when you work alone. Extroverted—you need a lot of interaction with people. Obnoxious—you're perfect for middle school ministry. Funny. A thinker. A doer. Organized. Spontaneous. Good at details. Good at imagining the big picture.)

What fires you up? (Do you have a unique passion for something? Does your heart beat faster for a cause? A need? What is it? World peace? A clean kitchen?)

Toward whom or what does your personal history and experience compel you? (Teenage moms? Divorcees? People gripped by addiction? Cancer survivors? Young leaders? Working moms? Children? Singles?) What have you been through?

What are your extra interests? (Are you a scrapbooker? Do you play sports? Do you sew? Paint? Love a good book? Throw a great party?) What do you love to do?

What are your skills? (How have you been trained professionally? What are you educated in? What do you do for a living? What skill have you acquired over the years?)

What need or people group do you weep for? (The homeless? Another country? Teens? Orphans? The poverty-stricken? Widows? The abused? The lost? The sick?)

Now, take those identity markers and look back at the list of spiritual gifts. At the very least, you can make an educated guess as to where you might fall. Showing mercy? Teaching? Contributing to the needs of others?

Remember, these gifts are umbrella terms encompassing a wealth of practical services under each one. The gift of teaching could be exercised with children, teens, women, single moms, widows, career girls, or any number of people. Women gifted with leadership could direct thousands of different ministry opportunities: A food pantry, a women's ministry, a greeter team, a mission trip. This is where gifts and passions unite. There are as many options as there are needs in this world.

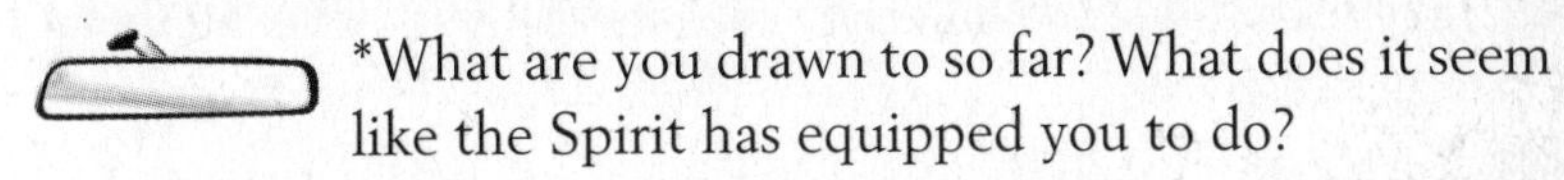

*What are you drawn to so far? What does it seem like the Spirit has equipped you to do?

It took me a few years to discover my calling. Now it seems obvious to me, but it took lots of trial and error until I finally said, "Aha!" The combination of passion, talent, history, and personality finally hit the right target. I teach women how to fall in love with God and His amazing Word. This is my niche. I know it as surely as I know that working in the nursery makes me neurotic. I'm just being honest.

However, my kids are taught by children's volunteers, who couldn't imagine serving anywhere else. My husband and I are served by the prayer team, who burn with passion for intercession. Fathers and sons serve side by side on the parking crew, which keeps me from wrecking my car every Sunday. I'm led to the throne each weekend by the most talented worship team. I get to celebrate the victories of the mission workers, who constantly cross the border to serve orphans and abused women.

When we all do our part, the church becomes the extension of God's hand. He is exalted, His people are served, the broken are cared for, and His fame is spread. It is a perfect design. If you're not sure where you fit, you can imitate my son and run around a bit until you find it. Run around in a ministry and test it out. If it's not quite right, run around in another one. Maybe you start a brand new ministry tailor-made for your skills. Experiment with service until you discover what you were created to do. Try anything but nothing.

Where will you start? What will you try first?

Here's how you'll know: You'll lie awake at night thinking about how to make your ministry stronger. You'll drive the people around you crazy talking about it. You'll constantly try to pull others into the fold. You'll read books and articles and make personal contacts that will reinforce your ministry. And at the end of the day, worn out from this level of kingdom work, you'll smile. For you, service will never again fall into the "responsibility" category. It will be your privilege.

Drape a towel over your arm.

The church needs you, Servant.

> From him the whole body, joined and held together by *every* supporting ligament, grows and builds itself up in love, as each part does its work. (Ephesians 4:16)

Girls, will you move toward the joy of serving? Will you give back to God the very gifts He gave you? Where are you being led today? Spend time with the Spirit in prayer asking for clarity on your niche and the courage to act on it.

DAY FOUR

The Clear Winner

A few months ago, Brandon and I and our friends, Mark and Stephanie, sat in the front row to watch Cirque du Soleil perform *Varekai*. Now I don't know if you've ever seen Cirque, but oh my land! The show is a series of mind-defying acts, such as a performer balancing on a rotating ball on a thumbtack with ten tiny Chinese boys standing on his head and stuff like that. That night, all the players came out for the most spectacular grand finale I have ever seen. People were flying and diving and flipping and trying to die all at the same time. Between the cast, the set design, the music, the costumes, and the tricks, I think I lost consciousness a couple of times there at the end.

As we were leaving, all four of us—grown adults I'll remind you—were talking over each other in a frenzy as we demonstrated various versions of our favorite acrobatic moments. We looked suspiciously like epileptic monkeys in fancy clothes. We absolutely did not care. We were so bowled over by what we'd seen that we lost all dignity. We were riding on the crescendo of *Varekai*, and walking upright and being sophisticated was simply not an option.

In terms of serving, Paul leaves us with a crescendo that absolutely mandates a strong response. Our carefully constructed dignity that keeps the wheels on, keeps everything civilized, gives way to an urgent intensity in light of his words.

After his two longest passages on spiritual gifts, Paul reaches a crescendo with the same message. Romans 12 and 1 Corinthians 12 explain gifts in the most detail: How we get them, what they look like, different types, how we use them, how we value them, how God values them. Details. And then it's as if Paul said, "You know what? Let's get down to the nitty-gritty."

Read his next words in Romans 12:9-21 and 1 Corinthians 12:31–13:7. How would you summarize the main point of each passage?

Romans 12:9-21

1 Corinthians 12:31–13:7

What does this have to do with spiritual gifts?

I think Paul was a smart guy. You know how sometimes you're neck deep explaining details, giving directions, loading down your listeners with stuff, then all of a sudden you realize you should back up and tell them why? "Because three boys on one bike means we'll end up in the ER again." "Because water running over the edge of the tub does not make an appropriate waterslide." "Because if I let a seven-year-old drive to Target, Mommy will go to jail." In other words, oh yeah, here's why you should even care about this. Here's why it matters.

*Without the fuel of love, how could the use of spiritual gifts get bogged down? What would the dangers be without this foundational motive?

I don't speak down from the mountaintop on this one, Girls. There might have been a couple of times in my history where I was heard saying something like: *I'm sick of doing all this work. I'm not being appreciated enough. I didn't sign up for all this maintenance. I'm unpaid, you know. This is cutting into my life. Why am I doing all the work? No one even knows how much I do.*

Sound familiar? This is service that has lost its source. Without love, serving will drain you and leave you bitter. That's why Paul said, "If I give all I possess to the poor and surrender my body to the flames, but have not love, I gain nothing" (1 Corinthians 13:3). On the other hand, when we fix our eyes on those we serve and love them with the strength God provides, there is nothing we won't do for them. Our reserves are renewed, and our urgency stays intact.

*Has serving ever drained you? If so, when and how?

Please believe me, Girls: I truly understand how love can get replaced with phone calls, e-mails, volunteer recruiting, volunteer replacing, glitches, confrontations, lack of resources, and so on. There have been times in my church ministry when I've been so preoccupied with sign-up lists, materials, teaching prep, and PowerPoint that I didn't think about the women I was serving one single time. That cycle simply cannot last. It voids our service of purpose, which drains our desire to continue.

Love is the most excellent way. It propels our patience, our fervor. Where organizing and planning and sacrificing lose momentum, love only grows stronger. When the faces of those you serve—the children, orphans, women, teens, parents, the poor, the lost, your church family—remain in your direct line of vision rather than shuffled off to the side, your desire is renewed daily.

So how do we maintain that kind of love? How can we keep its fires burning amid the phone calls and training meetings? Paul had some thoughts.

According to Romans 12:9-21 and 1 Corinthians 12:31–13:7, how would you say real love differs from love as a warm fuzzy feeling?

Love does not exist in a vacuum. It doesn't just happen. Real love is put on like a shield of purpose. Love digs down deep when your hard work is criticized. Love gains momentum as it clings to the good with intentional choices. Love is granted through a diligent prayer life. Love grows even stronger when you don't retaliate against someone who deserves it. Love blooms as it associates with the lowest ones; it's not too good to be found there.

What tangible strategy for real love will you include, starting today? Whom will you love?

This is the motive Jesus constantly boiled our earthly lives down to. When the grain was tossed and the chaff fell away, God's kingdom was always identified and distinguished by the love His followers had for Him and for each other. Period. Jesus stated clearly, "By this all men will know that you are my disciples, if you love one another" (John 13:35). Not "by the wisdom you spout out." Not "by the pretty prayers you deliver." Not even "by all that work you do."

He picked one distinction, and it was love.

We are most like Him when we love. We please Him most when we love. We serve His kingdom best when we love. Our gifts are fully realized for Him when we use them in love. This is the crescendo that informs all other areas of our spiritual lives. When pressed, Jesus said in Matthew 22:36-40:

1. Love God.
2. Love others.
3. Everything else falls under those.

*Why do you think Jesus said our love reveals our discipleship to onlookers more than anything else? What about all that other stuff we put so much value on?

For you, what other motives have crept into serving?

Is this supernatural? Definitely. This is Jesus-quality love we're talking about, the kind of love that begged God to forgive

His murderers as He hung suffering on the cross. This love strengthens our resolve to serve Him even as He hears, "I'm sick of doing this work." Jesus loves us with a patience and gentleness we'll never understand this side of heaven.

This brand of love can be ours. "God has poured out his love into our hearts by the Holy Spirit, whom he has given us" (Romans 5:5). At the same time the Spirit pours out your spiritual gift, He douses it with God's own love to ignite your service until it burns out of control. We must pray for God's love to remain full. Let's not dilute its concentration through distraction. Neither can we expect this love to burn consistently if we neglect the Spirit who maintains it.

The more we intentionally exhibit God's love to others, the more it takes permanent residence within. It's like those first few paces of a jog when your legs weigh five hundred pounds apiece. It feels strained and you question your decision to run. But as you force your steps to continue, you find a rhythm. Your strides lengthen out. You hit your groove. So it is with love. It is found while moving. It is an active phenomenon.

As Rob Bell, pastor of Mars Hill Bible Church, put it: "In our choice to serve, love wins." Girls, may love win in every paper you staple, in every e-mail you send, and in every neck you hug. May love be victorious with each need you sacrificially meet. May love conquer all reservations, distractions, and fear. When your days on this earth are over, may there be hundreds if not thousands who will say, "She really loved me. I'm sure I was her favorite."

Feeling empty? Ask God to fill you up with the strength of His love. Pray for fresh compassion. Ask the Spirit to help you move forward from the negatives that have drained your service. Commit to operating under the umbrella of love from this day forward.

DAY FIVE

Rest Stop

There are a few things I'd like to tell you. I want you to know how much I truly love you. I really do. Though I don't know your face, I know your journey. It's a lot like mine. I've dripped tears all over my laptop as God assured me of His work in all of our lives.

"I thank my God every time I remember you. In all my prayers for all of you, I always pray with joy because of your partnership in the gospel from the first day until now, being confident of this, that he who began a good work in you will carry it on to completion until the day of Christ Jesus" (Philippians 1:3-6). Thanks, Paul. That's exactly how I feel.

This good work on your significant Road Trip has carried you a long way. You've been traveling, moving forward. So have I. Now my Girlfriend Leslie and I are convinced that if large pools of information don't get summarized, the significance is vaporized within minutes (and that's not an indicator of any hard living we've done, because Leslie has never had a drop of alcohol in her entire life, and I thought that weird smell at a Willie Nelson concert was perfume). It just is what it is. So let's take a snapshot of your progress. For each of the following roads you journeyed, write the single largest lesson or truth you took away. Glance back over each week to remind you:

Week 1: The Road Trip of Togetherness

Week 2: The Road Trip of Identity

Week 3: The Road Trip of Faith

Week 4: The Road Trip of Discipleship

Week 5: The Road Trip of Contentment

Week 6: The Road Trip of Service

Those revelations were worth your time. They were worth the Spirit's time as He led you. Remember: This is a marathon, not a sprint. If you have moved out of neutral into drive in any of these areas it is cause for intense celebration. In fact, you and your Girlfriends should take a real road trip in honor of your spiritual travels. I'm pretty sure that's in the Bible somewhere. Like in Hezekiah.

Girls, let's press on together. It's a narrow road we travel, but it leads us to life. God gave us Girlfriends to journey with. What a bonus. We have His fascinating Word to show us exactly how to progress. The Holy Spirit makes sure we don't run on empty. Jesus made the journey possible. This is the Road Trip of a lifetime.

Buckle up.

> All sunshine and sovereign is GOD,
> generous in gifts and glory.
> He doesn't scrimp with his traveling companions.
> It's smooth sailing all the way with
> GOD-of-the-Angel Armies. (Psalm 84:11-12, MSG)

Leader's Guide

For this study, each woman will need:

1. A copy of *Road Trip*
2. A Bible (almost all of the references in the book come from the *New International Version*, but another version is fine).
3. A journal or notebook with lined paper.

Road Trip is a six-week study. Each week requires five days of work. Women will spend approximately thirty minutes on each day of Bible study.

Each week delves deeply into the Bible, what it meant as well as what it means now. All historical context is provided, but it's always helpful if the leader has some familiarity with the passages. I suggest having leaders stay at least a week ahead in the study in order to offer advance guidance if necessary. The ideal size for a small group is eight to twelve women.

In my church, the whole women's ministry gathers as a large group each week, and women divide into small groups at that time. This means that all the groups meet in the same building at the same time. I've found it helpful to have a leaders' meeting each week just before the large session. Twenty minutes together in prayer and discussion have addressed many issues before they came up in small groups. Leaders can discuss complicated questions and anticipate challenges in advance.

If the small groups meet in separate places, like homes, you can have a weekly online dialogue, or pair up leaders so they have a partner to encourage. Supported leaders are happier leaders.

The small group discussion should take sixty to ninety minutes, depending on the size and personality of the group. Feel free to supplement that time with worship, activities, or a large group session.

Each week, set the example by having your Bible and workbook open and ready. Begin each session with prayer, asking God to inhabit your conversation and increase your faith.

Have group members open their books to Days 1 through 4. The questions marked with an asterisk (*) are good discussion questions to pose. There are two to four of them marked in each day of study. Look ahead at the designated questions to prepare adequately for the discussion. Most of the questions selected involve the personal application of the study, but by all means keep bringing in the Scripture and history that set it up. Each week features a powerful story with fascinating details. Be sure to include them within the discussion. If your group obviously wants to pursue a different point, don't squash the Spirit's leading. Create an atmosphere of authenticity by voicing your own thoughts and struggles. Keep conversation moving, and work hard to include all four days in the discussion. If you aim to spend roughly fifteen minutes on each day's questions, Days 1 through 4 will take about an hour to cover.

When Days 1 through 4 have been discussed, refer to Day 5. As this was a personal prayer and journal activity, wrap up your conversation by asking, "What was the biggest thing you took away from this day? This week? What did the Spirit teach you in prayer and journaling?"

Close each discussion in prayer. This would be a great time to change up your prayer techniques each week.

- Try partner praying one week—two girls share immediate needs and pray over each other.
- You could lead the group in sentence prayer—only *one* or *two* sentences voiced at a time ("Thank you for teaching me how to walk forward this week." "Help me to accept my real identity.") Explain this technique first, and model it by beginning with a one-sentence prayer. When you think the girls are done, close in a brief final prayer.
- You could lead them through silent prayer using prompts from Scripture. For example, open to Psalm 66. Read verses 1-4 aloud and say, "Praise God for His awesome deeds in your life. Who has He been for you?" Give them two or three minutes to pray silently, then read verses 5-7 and say, "How has God delivered you? What has He done on your behalf?" Allow them to pray silently and continue through Scripture prompts as you see fit. This can be done with any passage you are drawn to or one that seems to uniquely fit your group.
- You could pray Scripture. Choose a passage like Psalm 33 or Exodus 15:1-18. Have each woman open her Bible to the chosen passage. Tell the group that you will read the whole passage aloud, then they will choose a line or phrase they'd like to pray again to God ("In your unfailing love you will lead the people you have redeemed."). Allow them to speak various verses randomly as God leads them. They might speak several times each over the course of the prayer. When it seems they are done, close briefly with a final prayer.
- If your group is small enough, you could try intercessory prayer. Take turns sentence praying over each group member individually. For example, put Jen in the middle. Each woman in turn prays one or two sentences over her. Think brief. Then move to Sarah and pray over her individually. It is a special way for your small group to connect with God in sweet intercession.

- Brainstorm with the other leaders on various prayer techniques. This is a wonderful place to teach creative prayer by example. Anything goes as long as God's name is honored.

Grand finale: Consider taking a day trip with your small group. What's close that your girls would love? A touristy town? A beautiful outdoor destination? Great shopping? This Road Trip has been all about spiritual growth and godly friendships. What better way to celebrate your victories than taking a little trip together?

I love group cohesion. My own personal small group has been together three years, and it just keeps getting better. The social and spiritual meld together. Karla Worley put it like this in her book *Traveling Together*:

> How can you, my friend in the faith, help me to become more like Christ? You can know me. You can be there. Hold me accountable for holy living. Encourage me to live the life of the Spirit. Model servanthood. Keep me active in worship and service. And you can do all this in the course of our days and years together, not just doing holy things, but understanding that all the things we do hold the possibility of the holy.[1]

Leaders, nurture friendships. Create authenticity. Make opportunities for real connection available. The longer you laugh and cry and pray together, the stronger this journey gets.

Notes

Week One: Road Trip

1. Matthew Henry, "Commentary on Matthew 11," *Matthew Henry Complete Commentary on the Whole Bible*, http://bible.crosswalk.com/Commentaries/MatthewHenryComplete/mhc-com.cgi?book=mt&chapter=011.
2. Matthew Henry, "Commentary on Matthew 7," *Matthew Henry Complete Commentary on the Whole Bible*, http://bible.crosswalk.com/Commentaries/MatthewHenryComplete/mhc-com.cgi?book=mt&chapter=007 (italics mine).
3. Karla Worley, *Traveling Together* (Birmingham, AL: New Hope Publishers, 2003), 19–20.

Week Two: Identity

1. "Jews and Samaritans," *Bible History Online*, http://www.bible-history.com/Samaritans/SAMARITANSJews_and_Samaritans.htm.
2. Kevin MacDonald, "What Makes Western Culture Unique?" *The Occidental Quarterly*, http://www.theoccidentalquarterly.com/vol2no2/km-unique.html.
3. "Women in Ancient Israel," *Bible History Online*, http://www.bible-history.com/court-of-women/women.html.

4. Bob Deffinbaugh, Th.M., "The New Testament Church—The Role of Women," *bible.org*, http://www.bible.org/page.asp?page_id=422#P672_132571.
5. B. A. Robinson, "The Status of Women in the Christian Gospels," *Ontario Consultants on Religious Tolerance*, http://www.religioustolerance.org/cfe_bibl.htm.

Week Three: Faith

1. Thomas Cahill, *The Gifts of the Jews* (New York: Nan A. Talese/Anchor Books, 1998), 11–15, 45, 59.
2. Cahill, 59.
3. Cahill, 58.

Week Four: Discipleship

1. Lois A. Tverberg, "Raise Up Many Disciples!" *En-Gedi Resource Center*, June 2002, http://www.egrc.net.
2. Mishnah, Pirke Avot 1:4; see also Tverberg.
3. Our Father Lutheran Church, Centennial, Colorado, "Caesarea Philippi," http://www.ourfatherlutheran.net/biblehomelands/galilee/banias.htm.

Week Five: Contentment

1. "Tarsus of Cilicia," *The Church of God: Daily Bible Study*, http://www.keyway.ca/htm2001/20011125.htm.
2. *NIV Study Bible* (Grand Rapids, MI: Zondervan, 2002), 1693.
3. "Gamaliel," *Bible History Online*, http://www.bible-history.com/isbe/G/GAMALIEL/.
4. *NIV Study Bible* (Grand Rapids, MI: Zondervan, 2002), 1660.
5. The Bible Knowledge Accelerator, "The Synagogue," *Bible History Online*, 1995–1996, http://www.bible-history.com/jesus/jesusThe_Synagogue.htm.

Week Six: Service

1. Thomas Cahill, *The Gifts of the Jews* (New York: Nan A. Talese/ Anchor Books, 1998), 108.
2. The Bible Knowledge Accelerator, "The Synagogue," *Bible History Online*, 1995–1996, http://www.bible-history.com/ jesus/jesusThe_Synagogue.htm.
3. "Feast of Pentecost," *Bible History Online*, http://www.bible -history.com/jesus/jesusuntitled00000335.htm.
4. Matthew Henry, "Commentary on 1 Corinthians 12," *Matthew Henry Complete Commentary on the Whole Bible*, http://bible .crosswalk.com/Commentaries/MatthewHenryComplete/mhc -com.cgi?book=1co&chapter=012.

Leader's Guide

1. Karla Worley, *Traveling Together* (Birmingham, AL: New Hope Publishers, 2003), 43.

About the Author

Jen has partnered with her husband, Brandon, in full-time ministry for eleven years while keeping her vow never to wear suntan pantyhose and white flats. If you catch her in either of those, please contact her Girlfriends immediately so they can stage an intervention. Although she has purchased either a new outfit or new shoes every single time she's been invited as a speaker, she is still happily married after eleven years (to the same man). Jen lives in beautiful Austin, Texas, but has somehow avoided becoming a runner, a bicyclist, a granola, or an earth-conscious recycler.

Jen intensely loves God, Jesus, her church, Scripture, writing, teaching, women, and finding the funny and profound in all these things. She surrounds herself with friends who, if not technically insane, are at least reassuringly dysfunctional. If nothing else, their lives provide amusing anecdotes should her own family ever become normal. However, her three kids—Gavin, Sydney Beth, and Caleb—have definitively squashed any notion that her life will ever be normal (see all stories included in this book). She recently crossed the threshold into her thirties, feigning indifference, where she now happily resides as a pretend grown-up.

Her first book, *A Modern Girl's Guide to Bible Study*, is also published by NavPress. Also out is her Bible study *Tune In: Hearing God's Voice Through the Static.* Jen has two more Bible studies in the works.

For more information on Jen's ministry or to schedule her for your conference, retreat, or speaking engagement, go to www.jenhatmaker.com. You can also write to her at 7509 Callbram Lane, Austin, Texas 78736.